MW01097246

Crock Pot Express Cookbook

Easy, Healthy and Tasty Crock Pot Express Recipes for Great Food

Dave Zinman

Copyright © 2017
Dave Zinman

All rights reserved worldwide.

ISBN: 978-1981499021

You may not reproduce or transmitte any part of the book, in any form or by any means, electronic or mechanical, including photocopying, recording or by any information storage and retrieval system, without written permission from the publisher or author, except for the inclusion of brief quotations in a review.

Warning-Disclaimer

The purpose of this book is to educate and entertain. The author or publisher does not guarantee that anyone following the techniques, suggestions, tips, ideas, or strategies will become successful. The author and publisher shall have neither liability or responsibility to anyone with respect to any loss or damage caused, or alleged to be caused, directly or indirectly by the information contained in this book.

Contents

Introduction

If you are looking for, whipping up delicious, nutritious and tasty meals with a single touch of a button, then you need a multi-cooker that can cook as a slow cooker as well as a pressure cooker. The Crock Pot Express does just that - it serves not only as a slow cooker but also as a fast and efficient electric pressure cooker. Spend less time in your kitchen and enjoy the company of your loved ones while The Crock Pot Express takes care of your dinner.

The Crock Pot Express combines the functions of a pressure cooker and a slow cooker making it the perfect multi-cooker for your kitchen. It and can also steam, sauté or brown, all in a single kitchen appliance. A little too much information for you? Don't worry, as this cookbook will guide you through the process of taking advantage of your Crock Pot Express.

It encompasses a wide variety of recipes, very easy to follow and most importantly, very easy to cook in your Crock Pot Express multi-cooker.

Before you start to cook, take a loot at the control buttons and how to use them.

Slow Cook

It allows you to use your Crock Pot Express as slow cooker. Perfect for a meal when you arrive home.

Meat/Stew

The program allows you to cook a lot of foods, including meat and stews. It's also great for quick appetizers or side dishes.

Steam

To be used with steaming rack or basket. Perfect for fish, vegetables or something light and quick.

Brown & Sauté

Use to sear or brown meat or to sauté some veggies before the actual cooking process.

Rice/Risotto

This setting is to steam or boil rice or risotto. Can be used for some Desserts as well.

Poultry

This setting is to be used for chicken, duck or turkey meals.

Beans/Chili

Use for delicious beans or chilies.

Soup

Great function that will cook your soups for you.

Multigrain

This setting allows you to cook grains in quick and effortless way.

Yogurt

This setting allows you to prepare delicious and healthy home-made yogurt.

Start/Stop

As it name suggests, this setting start or stops the cooking process.

Now that you have the basics, let's start cooking!

Poultry

Chicken in Beer Sauce

(Prep + Cook Time: 40 minutes / Servings: 4)

Ingredients:

1 ½ pounds Chicken Breasts
10 ounces Beer
1 cup chopped Green Onions
1 ¼ cup Greek Yogurt
⅓ cup Arrowroot
½ tsp Sage
2 tsp dried Thyme
2 tsp dried Rosemary
2 tbsp Olive Oil

Directions:

Heat the oil in your Power Crock Pot Express on SAUTÉ.

Add onions and cook for 2 minutes. Coat the chicken with the arrowroot.

Add the chicken to the cooker and cook until browned on all sides.

Pour the beer over and bring the mixture to a boil.

Stir in the herbs and cook on MEAT/STEW for 30 minutes.

Stir in the yogurt before serving.

Fennel Chicken Breast

(Prep + Cook Time: 25 minutes / Servings: 8)

Ingredients:

2 pounds Chicken Breasts, boneless and skinless
1 cup chopped Celery
1 cup chopped Fennel
2 ¼ cup Chicken Stock
Salt and Pepper, to taste

Directions:

Chop the chicken into small pieces and place in your Crock Pot Express.

Add the remaining ingredients and stir well to combine.

Set your Crock Pot Express to POULTRY and cook for 15 minutes. Release the pressure naturally. Season with salt and pepper, to taste.

Black Currant and Lemon Chicken

(Prep + Cook Time: 20 minutes / Servings: 6)

Ingredients:

1 ½ pound Chicken Breasts
1/3 cup Red Currants
2 Garlic Cloves, minced
6 Lemon Slices
1 cup chopped Scallions
1 cup Black Olives, pitted
2 tbsp Canola Oil
¼ tsp Pepper
1 tsp Coriander Seeds
1 tsp Cumin
¼ tsp Salt
2 ¼ cup Water

Directions:

Preheat your Crock Pot Express to SAUTÉ and heat the canola oil in it.

Add scallions, coriander, and garlic and sauté for 30 seconds.

Add the chicken and top with olives and red currants.

Sprinkle the salt and pepper over, arrange the lemon slices on top, and pour the water over.

Close the lid and press START/STOP. Cook the chicken for 15 minutes. Release the pressure naturally.

Creamy Chicken and Green Beans

(Prep + Cook Time: 35 minutes / Servings: 4)

Ingredients:

4 boneless and skinless Chicken Breasts, frozen
2 cups frozen Green Beans
14 ounces Cornbread Stuffing
1 tsp Cajun Seasoning
1 cup Chicken Broth

Directions:

Combine the chicken and broth in the Crock Pot Express, close the lid, and cook on MEAT/STEW for 18 minutes.

Allow the pressure to release naturally.

Add the green beans, close the lid again, and cook for 2 more minutes on MEAT/STEW.

Stir in the cornbread stuffing and Cajun seasoning and cook for another 5 minutes. Release the pressure naturally.

Balsamic Chicken Thighs with Pears

(Prep + Cook Time: 30 minutes / Servings: 6)

Ingredients:

6 large Chicken Thighs
½ cup chopped Sweet Onions
3 small Pears, peeled and sliced
2 tbsp Balsamic Vinegar
3 tsp Butter
1 cup Chicken Broth
1 tsp Cayenne Pepper
Salt and Pepper, to taste

Directions:

Melt the butter in your Crock Pot Express on SAUTÉ.

Add chicken and sprinkle with the spices. Brown on all sides. Stir in the remaining ingredients.

Close the lid and press START/STOP. Cook for 20 minutes.

Release the pressure naturally.

Cheesy Drumsticks in Marinara Sauce

(Prep + Cook Time: 35 minutes / Servings: 4)

Ingredients:

4 Chicken Drumsticks
1 cup Sour Cream
1 ¾ cup Marinara Sauce
1 cup grated Cheddar Cheese
½ Butter Stick
1 tsp chipotle Powder
½ tsp Rosemary
Salt and Pepper, to taste

Directions:

Melt the butter in your Crock Pot Express on BEANS/CHILI.

Add marinara, chipotle, rosemary, and chicken.

Season with salt and pepper. Close the lid and press START/STOP button. Cook for 20 minutes.

Press STOP and release the pressure naturally. Stir in the cheese and sour cream.

Tomato and Coconut Milk Chicken with Almonds

(Prep + Cook Time: 25 minutes / Servings: 6)

Ingredients:

3 pounds Chicken Breasts, boneless and skinless
2 cans of Coconut Milk
12 ounces canned Tomato Paste
2 cups canned Tomatoes, undrained

½ cup sliced Almonds
1 ½ Onions, chopped
1 tbsp Butter
2 tsp Paprika
1 ½ tsp Cayenne Powder
1 tsp Garlic Powder
Salt and Pepper, to taste

Directions:

Melt the butter in your Crock Pot Express on SAUTÉ.

Add the onions and spices and sauté for 2 minutes. Add the tomatoes, tomato paste, and coconut milk. Add chicken and close the lid. Cook for 12 minutes.

Press STOP, release the pressure naturally, and stir in the almonds.

Sweet and Gingery Whole Chicken

(Prep + Cook Time: 60 minutes / Servings: 6)

Ingredients:

1 medium Whole Chicken
1 Green Onion, minced
2 tbsp Sugar
1 tbsp grated Ginger
2 tsp Soy Sauce
¼ cup White Wine
½ cup Chicken Broth
1 ½ tbsp Olive Oil
2 tsp Salt
¼ tsp Pepper

Directions:

Heat the olive oil in your Express Crock on SAUTÉ.

Season the chicken with the sugar and half the salt and pepper; brown on all sides.

Whisk together the wine, broth, soy sauce, and remaining salt, in the Multi-Cooker. Add the chicken and seal the lid.

Press START and cook for 35 minutes. Release the pressure naturally.

BBQ Pulled Turkey

(Prep + Cook Time: 100 minutes / Servings: 4)

Ingredients:

2 pounds Turkey Breasts, boneless and skinless
½ cup Beer
1 ½ tbsp Oil

Sauce:

2 tbsp Honey
¼ cup Apple Cider Vinegar
1 tsp Liquid Smoke
2 tsp Sriracha
1 tsp Garlic Powder
1 tsp Onion Powder
½ cup Mustard
1 tbsp Worcestershire Sauce
2 tbsp Honey
1 tsp Mustard Powder
2 tbsp Olive Oil

Directions:

Heat the oil in your Crock Pot Express on SAUTÉ.

Add the turkey and brown on all sides.

Whisk together all the sauce ingredients in a small bowl.

Add beer and sauce to the Crock Pot Express. Stir to combine.

Close the lid and cook for 70 minutes.

Release the pressure naturally.

Transfer the turkey to a plate and shred with two forks.

Set the Crock Pot Express back to BROWN/SAUTÉ and cook until the sauce is reduced and thickened.

Return the turkey and stir to coat well.

Habanero Turkey Breasts

(Prep + Cook Time: 30 minutes / Servings: 6)

Ingredients:

2 pounds Turkey Breasts
6 tbsp Habanero Sauce
½ cup Tomato Puree
⅓ cup Maple Syrup
1 ½ cups Water
½ tsp Cumin
1 tsp Smoked Paprika
Salt and Pepper, to taste

Directions:

Pour the water in your Crock Pot Express and place the turkey in the steaming basket.

Close the lid, select POULTRY, and cook for 15 minutes.

Press STOP and release the pressure naturally.

Discard the cooking liquid.

Shred the turkey within the pot and add the remaining ingredients.

Cook on POULTRY with the lid off for a few minutes, or until thickened.

Hot and Buttery Chicken Wings

(Prep + Cook Time: 20 minutes / Servings: 4)

Ingredients:

16 Chicken Wings, frozen
1 cup Hot Sauce by choice
2 tbsp Butter

Directions:

Combine all the ingredients in your Crock Pot Express.

Close the lid and choose the MEAT/STEW function.

Cook for 15 minutes. Press STOP and release the pressure naturally.

Turkey with Tomatoes and Red Beans

(Prep + Cook Time: 20 minutes / Servings: 6)

Ingredients:

1 pound Turkey Breasts, cut into cubes
16 ounces canned Stewed Tomatoes
16 ounces canned red Kidney Beans, drained
2 cups Chicken Stock
1/3 cup Sour Cream
2 tbsp chopped Parsley

Directions:

Place the beans, tomatoes, turkey, stock, and sour cream in your Crock Pot Express. Season with salt and pepper. Choose the MEAT/STEW function and cook for 15 minutes.

Release the pressure naturally. Serve topped with chopped parsley and enjoy.

Orange and Cranberry Turkey Wings

(Prep + Cook Time: 40 minutes / Servings: 4)

Ingredients:

1 pound Turkey Wings
1/3 cup Orange Juice
1 stick of Butter
2 cups Cranberries
2 Onions, sliced
2 cups Veggie Stock
½ tsp Cayenne Pepper
Salt and Pepper, to taste

Directions:

Melt the butter in the Crock Pot Express on BROWN/SAUTÉ.

Add the turkey wings, season with salt, pepper, and cayenne pepper, and cook until browned.

Stir in the remaining ingredients and close the lid. Cook for 25 minutes. Release the pressure naturally.

Chicken and Red Potatoes in Pesto Sauce

(Prep + Cook Time: 25 minutes / Servings: 4)

Ingredients:

2 pounds Chicken Thighs, boneless and skinless
8 medium Red Potatoes
1 tsp Lemon Juice
1/3 cup Pesto Sauce
1 Sweet Onion, sliced
½ cup Chicken Broth

Directions:

In a bowl, coat the chicken with the pesto sauce and lemon juice.

Place the remaining ingredients in the Crock Pot Express and add the chicken.

Select MEAT/STEW, close the lid, and select START.

Cook for 10 minutes.

Release the pressure naturally.

Curry and Coconut Milk Chicken

(Prep + Cook Time: 25 minutes / Servings: 4)

Ingredients:

1 pound boneless and skinless Chicken Breasts
½ cup Coconut Milk
½ tsp Turmeric
2 tsp Curry Paste
1 tsp Brown Sugar
¼ tsp Pepper

Directions:

Chop the chicken into cubes and place them in the Express Crock Pot. Stir in the remaining ingredients.

Seletct POULTRY, and cook for 25 minutes.

Allow the pressure to release naturally.

Mustard and Lime Goose

(Prep + Cook Time: 30 minutes / Servings: 4)

Ingredients:

1 pound skinless and boneless Goose Meat, cut into cubes
½ cup White Wine
1 tbsp Dijon Mustard
1 tbsp minced Garlic
2 tbsp Oil
Juice from 1 Lime
¼ tsp Thyme
¼ tsp Oregano
Salt and Pepper, to taste
¼ cup Chicken Broth

Directions:

Heat the oil in your Crock Pot Express on SAUTÉ.

Add the goose meat and brown for 5 minutes.

Add the remaining ingredients and stir to coat well.

Close the lid and cook for 10 minutes.

Release the pressure naturally.

Transfer the goose to a plate.

Cook the sauce with the lid off for a few minutes, until thickened.

Add the meat and stir to coat well.

Creamy Chicken with Mushrooms and Baby Carrots

(Prep + Cook Time: 30 minutes / Servings: 6)

Ingredients:

6 Chicken Breasts, boneless and skinless
1 Sweet Onion, diced
8 ounces Mushrooms, sliced
1 can Cream of Mushroom Soup
1 pound Baby Carrots

1 tbsp Butter
1 tbsp Olive Oil
2 tbsp Heavy Cream

Directions:

Add oil and butter in your Crock Pot Express and melt it on BROWN/SAUTÉ until melted.

Add onions and mushrooms and cook for 3 minutes with the lid on. Release the pressure naturally and add the carrots, chicken, and mushroom soup.

Close the lid and cook for 8 minutes on RICE/RISOTTO.

Transfer the mushrooms, chicken, and carrots to a plate.

Stir in the heavy cream and cook the sauce until it thickens.

Serve the chicken and veggies drizzled with the sauce.

Turkey Thighs in Fig Sauce

(Prep + Cook Time: 35 minutes / Servings: 4)

Ingredients:

4 pound Turkey Thighs
1 cup sliced Carrots
1 Onion, chopped
4 Potatoes, chopped
½ cup Balsamic Vinegar
12 dried Figs, halved
1 cup Chicken Broth
½ Celery Stalk, diced
Salt and Pepper, to taste

Directions:

Place the veggies and turkey in your Crock Pot Express. Whisk together the remaining ingredients in a bowl and pour the mixture over the turkey. Stir in the figs.

Close the lid, choose the POULTRY mode, and cook for 15 minutes. Release the pressure naturally. Transfer the figs, turkey, and veggies to a plate.

Strain the sauce and pour over the turkey and veggies.

Turkey Meatloaf

(Prep + Cook Time: 30 minutes / Servings: 4)

Ingredients:

1 ½ pounds ground Turkey
1 Carrot, grated
1 Onion, diced
1 Celery Stalk, diced
½ cup Breadcrumbs
1 Egg
3 tbsp Ketchup
1 tsp minced Garlic
½ tsp Thyme
¼ tsp Oregano
¼ tsp Salt
¼ tsp Pepper
1 tsp Worcestershire Sauce
1 ½ cup Water

Directions:

Pour the water in your Crock Pot Express. Combine all of the remaining ingredients in a large bowl.

Grease a pan with cooking spray and press the mixture in it. Lower the trivet and place the pan inside your Crock Pot Express.

Close the lid and cook on POULTRY for 15 minutes.

Release the pressure naturally.

Balsamic Orange Chicken

(Prep + Cook Time: 30 minutes / Servings: 4)

Ingredients:

4 Chicken Breasts, boneless and skinless
2 tbsp Balsamic Vinegar
1 cup Orange Juice Concentrate
1 tsp Thyme

½ tsp Rosemary
1 Garlic Clove, minced
Pinch of Black Pepper

Directions:

Rub the chicken with pepper, rosemary, thyme, and garlic.

Place it in the Crock Pot Express.

In a bowl, whisk together the orange concentrate and vinegar. Pour the mixture over the chicken. Press POULTRY and cook for 20 minutes. Allow the pressure to release naturally.

Honey and Ketchup Chicken

(Prep + Cook Time: 35 minutes / Servings: 4)

Ingredients:

4 Chicken Breasts
1/3 cup Ketchup
1 cup Honey
1/3 cup Soy Sauce
1 Onion, diced
2 tbsp Cornstarch
5 tbsp Water
2 tbsp Olive Oil
Salt and Pepper, to taste

Directions:

Cut the chicken into strips.

Whisk together the honey, ketchup, oil, soy sauce, and some salt and pepper.

Place the chicken and mixture in the Crock Pot Express and stir to combine. Select POULTRY and cook for 17 minutes Release the pressure naturally and transfer the chicken to a plate.

Stir in the water and cornstarch and cook the sauce for a few minutes with the lid off, until thickened.

Return the chicken to the Crock Pot Express.

Simple Garlicky Goose

(Prep + Cook Time: 70 minutes / Servings: 5)

Ingredients:

½ medium Goose, cut into pieces
1 Onion, chopped
12 ounces canned Mushroom Soup
2 tsp minced Garlic
3 ½ cups Water
Salt and Pepper, to taste

Directions:

Place the water, goose, onion, and garlic in your Crock Pot Express.

Close the lid and cook on MEAT/STEW for an hour.

Stir in the mushroom soup and season with salt and pepper.

Cook for 5 minutes with the lid off.

Spicy Creamy Yogurt Chicken

(Prep + Cook Time: 25 minutes / Servings: 4-8)

Ingredients:

8 Chicken Thighs
¾ cup Yogurt
¾ cup Heavy Cream
½ cup Butter
28 ounces canned Tomatoes, drained
2 Jalapeno Peppers, chopped
1 tsp grated Ginger
2 tbsp Cumin
2 tbsp Garam Masala
2 tbsp Water
2 tbsp Cornstarch

Directions:

Place the ginger, tomatoes, and jalapenos in a blender and blend until smooth.

Melt the butter in your Crock Pot Express and brown the thighs on BROWN/ SAUTÉ.

Add the spices, heavy cream, and yogurt.

Pour the tomato sauce over.

Press POULTRY, close the lid and cook for 15 minutes.

Release the pressure naturally.

Whisk together the water and cornstarch and stir the mixture into the Crock Pot Express.

Cook for 2 more minutes.

Thyme and Lemon Drumsticks

(Prep + Cook Time: 35 minutes / Servings: 4)

Ingredients:

4 Chicken Drumsticks
1 Onion, sliced
½ cup canned diced Tomatoes
2 tsp dried Thyme
1 tsp Lemon Zest
2 tbsp Lemon Juice
1 tbsp Olive Oil
Salt and Pepper, to taste

Directions:

Heat the olive oil in your Crock Pot Express on BROWN/SAUTÉ.

Add the drumsticks and brown for a few minutes.

Stir in the remaining ingredients.

Press POULTRY and close the lid.

Cook for 15 minutes.

Release the pressure naturally.

Smoked Paprika Chicken Legs

(Prep + Cook Time: 30 minutes / Servings: 4)

Ingredients:

4 Chicken Legs (about 8-ounce each)
1 Onion, chopped
1 Tomato, chopped
½ cup Sour Cream
½ cup Chicken Broth
1 tbsp Olive Oil
2 tsp Smoked Paprika
½ tsp Garlic Powder
¼ tsp Salt
¼ tsp Pepper

Directions:

Season the chicken with salt, pepper, garlic powder, and smoked paprika.

Heat the oil in your Crock Pot Express on BROWN/SAUTÉ and brown the chicken legs on all sides.

Stir in the remaining ingredients and close the lid.

Cook for 15 minutes.

Release the pressure naturally.

Bacon and Cheese Shredded Chicken

(Prep + Cook Time: 40 minutes / Servings: 4)

Ingredients:

4 Chicken Breasts
8 ounces Cream Cheese
2 cups shredded Cheddar Cheese
¼ cup chopped Scallion
4 ounces chopped Bacon
1 cup Mayonnaise
½ cup Chicken Broth
2 tsp Ranch Seasoning

Directions:

Select BROWN/SAUTÉ.

Add the bacon and cook until crispy, a few minutes.

Transfer the bacon to a plate.

Add chicken, broth, cream cheese, and ranch dressing. Close the lid and cook for 15 minutes. Release the pressure naturally.

Shred the chicken with two forks inside the Crock Pot Express.

Stir in the remaining ingredients and cook for 2 more minutes.

Allow the pressure to release naturally and serve as desired.

Pineapple and Coconut Chicken Drumsticks

(Prep + Cook Time: 25 minutes / Servings: 4)

Ingredients:

4 Chicken Drumsticks
1 cup chopped Pineapple
½ cup Coconut Milk
½ cup Tomato Sauce
2 tbsp Brown Sugar
2 tbsp Apple Cider Vinegar
1 tbsp Lime Juice
2 tbsp Water
Salt and Pepper, to taste

Directions:

Whisk together all the sauce ingredients in a bowl.

Place the chicken drumsticks and pineapple in the Crock Pot Express and pour the sauce over.

Close the lid, set your Crock Pot Express to POULTRY and cook for 15 minutes.

Allow the pressure to release naturally.

Mexican Turkey Breasts

(Prep + Cook Time: 35 minutes / Servings: 4)

Ingredients:

24 ounces Turkey Breasts, frozen
1 cup shredded Mozzarella Cheese
1 cup mild Salsa
1 cup Tomato Sauce
3 tbsp Lime Juice
Salt and Pepper, to taste

Directions:

Place the tomato sauce, salsa, lime juice, and turkey in your Crock Pot Express.

Close the lid, and cook on POULTRY for 15 minutes. Do a natural pressure release.

Shred the turkey inside the Crock Pot Express and stir in the cheese. Cook for another minute on POULTRY.

Garlic and Thyme Chicken

(Prep + Cook Time: 40 minutes / Servings: 4-6)

Ingredients:

3 ½ pound Whole Chicken
1 tbsp dried Thyme
Juice from 1 Lemon
3 Garlic Cloves
2 cups Chicken Broth
½ tsp Pepper
½ tsp Salt
1 tbsp Olive Oil

Directions:

Season the chicken with salt, pepper, and thyme.

Heat the olive oil in your Crock Pot Express on BROWN/SAUTÉ and brown the chicken with the breast-side down.

Add garlic and cook for 30 more seconds.

Pour the broth and lemon juice around (not over!) the chicken.

Select MEAT/STEW and cook for 25 minutes.

Release the pressure naturally.

Basil and Oregano Duck Breasts

(Prep + Cook Time: 30 minutes / Servings: 4)

Ingredients:

18 ounces Duck Breasts
1 tsp dried Oregano
1 tsp dried Basil
1 tsp Garlic Powder
1 ¼ cups Chicken Broth
1 tbsp Coconut Oil
Salt and Pepper, to taste

Directions:

Season the duck breasts with the herbs and spices.

Melt the coconut oil in your Crock Pot Express on BROWN/SAUTÉ.

Add the duck and cook for a few minutes, until browned.

Pour the chicken broth over, select MEAT/STEW and close the lid.

Cook for 15 minutes.

Allow the pressure to release naturally and serve.

Pork

Creamy Pork in a Mushroom and Root Beer Sauce

(Prep + Cook Time: 50 minutes / Servings: 8)

Ingredients:

3 pounds Pork Roast
8 ounces Mushroom, sliced
12 ounces Root Beer
10 ounces Cream of Mushroom Soup
1 package of Dry Onion Soup

Directions:

Whisk together the mushroom soup, dry onion soup mix, and root beer in the Crock Pot Express. Add the mushrooms and pork.

Close the lid and set it to MEAT/STEW. Cook for 40 minutes.

Let sit for 5 minutes before doing a quick pressure release.

Pork Butt with Mushrooms and Celery

(Prep + Cook Time: 35 minutes / Servings: 4)

Ingredients:

1 pound Pork Butt, sliced
2 cups sliced Mushrooms
1 ½ cup chopped Celery Stalk
1/3 cup White Wine
1 tsp minced Garlic
½ cup Chicken Broth
½ tsp Salt
¼ tsp Pepper

Directions:

Coat your Crock Pot Express with some cooking spray and heat to BROWN/ SAUTÉ.

Add the pork slices and cook for a few minutes until browned.

Add mushrooms and celery and stir in the remaining ingredients.

Press MEAT/STEW and close the lid.

Cook for 20 minutes. Release the pressure naturally.

Pork Chops with Brussel Sprouts

(Prep + Cook Time: 30 minutes / Servings: 4)

Ingredients:

4 Pork Chops
½ pound Brussel Sprouts
1/3 cup Sparkling Wine
1 ½ cups Beef Stock
2 Shallots, chopped
1 tbsp Olive Oil
1 cup chopped Celery Stalk
1 tbsp Coriander
¼ tsp Salt
¼ tsp Pepper

Directions:

Heat the olive oil in your Crock Pot Express on BROWN/SAUTÉ. Add the pork chops and cook until browned on all sides. Stir in the remaining ingredients.

Selecet MEAT/STEW, close the lid and cook for 15 minutes.

Press STOP and release the pressure naturally.

Braised Red Cabbage and Bacon

(Prep + Cook Time: 20 minutes / Servings: 8)

Ingredients:

1 pound Red Cabbage, chopped
8 Bacon Slices, chopped
1 ½ cups Beef Broth
2 tbsp Butter
½ tsp Salt and pepper

Directions:

Add the bacon slices in your Crock Pot Express, set it to BEANS/CHILI, and cook for 5 minutes, or until crispy.

Stir in the cabbage, salt, pepper, and butter.

Press STEAM function.

Cook for 10 minutes and release the pressure naturally.

Pineapple Pork Loin

(Prep + Cook Time: 30 minutes / Servings: 6)

Ingredients:

2 ½ pounds Pork Loin, cut into 6 equal pieces
16 ounces canned Pineapple
1 tbsp Brown Sugar
1 tbsp Cornstarch Slurry
2 tbsp Olive Oil
½ cup Tomato Paste
1 cup sliced Onions
½ tsp grated Ginger
½ tsp Garlic Salt
½ tsp Pepper
1/3 cup Tamari
¼ cup Rice Wine Vinegar

Directions:

Heat the oil in your Crock Pot Express set to BROWN/SAUTÉ. Add onions and cook for a few minutes.

Add the pork and stir in the rest of the ingredients.

Select MEAT/STEW, close the lid and cook for 20 minutes.

Release the pressure naturally.

Stir in the cornstarch slurry and let simmer until thickened.

Pork Loin and Sweet Potatoes

(Prep + Cook Time: 35 minutes / Servings: 6)

Ingredients:

1 1/3 pounds Pork Loin, cubed
1 pound Sweet Potatoes, cut into cubes
½ cup chopped Bell Pepper
1 Large Sweet Onion, chopped
1 cup Cream of Mushroom Soup
Salt and Pepper, to taste

Directions:

Add the pork loin in your Crock Pot Express and brown them on all sides on BROWN/SAUTÉ.

Add onions, peppers, and potatoes and cook for 5 more minutes.

Pour the soup over and season with salt and pepper.

Press MEAT/STEW, close the lid and cook for 20 minute.

Press STOP and release the pressure naturally.

Pork Cutlets with Baby Carrots

(Prep + Cook Time: 30 minutes / Servings: 4)

Ingredients:

1 pound Pork Cutlets
1 pound Baby Carrots
1 Onion, sliced
1 tbsp Butter
1/3 cup Apple Cider
1 tsp Garlic Powder
Salt and Pepper, to taste

Directions:

Season the pork with salt and pepper.

Melt the butter in your Crock Pot Express on BROWN/SAUTÉ and brown the pork on all sides.

Add carrots and onions and cook for 2 more minutes.

Stir in the apple cider, garlic powder, and sprinkle salt and pepper over.

SELECT MEAT/STEW, close the lid and cook for 15 minutes.

Release the pressure naturally.

Apple Cider Pork Shoulder

(Prep + Cook Time: 50 minutes / Servings: 4)

Ingredients:

1 pound Pork Shoulder
1/3 cup Apple Cider
¾ cup Water
3 tsp Olive Oil
1 tsp Cayenne Pepper
1 tbsp Sesame Oil
Salt and Pepper, to taste

Directions:

Heat the oil in your Crock Pot Express on BROWN/SAUTÉ.

Season the pork with cayenne pepper, salt, and pepper.

Add to the Crock Pot Express and sear on all sides for a few minutes. Stir in the remaining ingredients.

Close the lid and press START/STOP. Select SOUP and cook for 40 minutes. Release the pressure naturally.

Ground Pork with Cabbage and Tomatoes

(Prep + Cook Time: 25 minutes / Servings: 6)

Ingredients:

1 1/3 pounds Ground Pork
1 cup shredded Cabbage
½ cup chopped Celery
2 Red Onions, chopped
2 large Tomatoes, chopped

1 Carrot, shredded
1 Bell Pepper, chopped
1/3 tsp Cumin
1 tsp Red Pepper Flakes
Salt and Pepper, to taste

Directions:

Coat the Crock Pot Express with cooking spray and cook the ground pork until browned on BROWN/SAUTÉ.

Stir in the remaining ingredients. Select MEAT/STEW, close the lid and cook for 15 minutes.

Allow the pressure to release naturally.

Ground Pork and Sauerkraut

(Prep + Cook Time: 25 minutes / Servings: 6)

Ingredients:

1 ¼ pounds Ground Pork
4 cups shredded Sauerkraut
1 cup Tomato Puree
½ cup Chicken Stock
1 Red Onion, chopped
2 Garlic Cloves, minced
2 Bay Leaves
Salt and Pepper, to taste

Directions:

Set your Crock Pot Express to BROWN/SAUTÉ.

Add the onions, garlic, and pork.

Cook until browned.

Stir in the remaining ingredients and season with salt and pepper. Choose MEAT/STEW, close the lid and cook for 15 minutes.

Press STOP and release the pressure naturally. Discard the bay leaves.

Sage Pork Butt and Yams

(Prep + Cook Time: 20 minutes / Servings: 4)

Ingredients:

1 pound Pork Butt, cut into 4 equal pieces
1 pound Yams, diced
2 tsp Butter
¼ tsp Thyme
1 ½ tsp Sage
1 ½ cups Beef Broth
Salt and Pepper, to taste

Directions:

Season the pork with thyme, sage, salt, and pepper.

Melt the butter in your Crock Pot Express on BROWN/SAUTÉ.

Add the pork and cook until browned for a few minutes.

Add the yams and pour the broth over.

Select MEAT/STEW, close the lid and cook for 15 minutes.

Allow the pressure to release naturally and serve.

Pork Ribs in a Walnut Sauce

(Prep + Cook Time: 30 minutes / Servings: 4)

Ingredients:

1 pound Pork Ribs
¼ cup chopped Roasted Walnuts
4 Garlic Cloves, minced
1 ½ cups Beef Broth
2 tbsp Apple Cider Vinegar
3 tbsp Butter
½ tsp Red Pepper Flakes
1 tsp Sage
Salt and Pepper, to taste

Directions:

Melt the butter in your Crock Pot Express on BROWN/SAUTÉ.

Season the ribs with salt, pepper, sage, and pepper flakes.

Brown them on all sides, about 5 minutes in total.

Stir in the remaining ingredients.

Select MEAT/STEW, close the lid and cook for 15 minutes.

Release the pressure naturally.

Serve the ribs drizzled with the sauce.

Pork Meatloaf with Ketchup

(Prep + Cook Time: 70 minutes / Servings: 4)

Ingredients:

1 pound ground Sausage
1 pound ground Pork
1 cup cooked Rice
3/4 cup Milk
½ tsp Cayenne Powder
½ tsp Marjoram
2 Eggs, beaten
2 Garlic Cloves, minced
1 Onion, diced

Topping:

2 tbsp Brown Sugar
1 cup Ketchup

Directions:

Place all of the meatloaf ingredients in a bowl and mix with your hands to combine.

Grease the Express Crock with cooking spray. Press the meatloaf mixture into the multi-cooker.

Whisk together the ketchup and sugar and pour over the meatloaf. Close the lid and cook on MEAT/STEW for 60 minutes.

Tangy Pork in a Tomato and Sour Cream Sauce

(Prep + Cook Time: 45 minutes / Servings: 6)

Ingredients:

1 ½ pounds Pork Shoulder cut into pieces
2 Onions, chopped
1 ½ cups Sour Cream
1 cup Tomato Puree
½ tbsp Coriander
¼ tsp Cumin
¼ tsp Cayenne Pepper
1 tsp minced Garlic
Salt and Pepper, to taste

Directions:

Coat the Crock Pot Express with some cooking spray and brown the pork on BROWN/SAUTÉ.

Add onions and garlic and cook for 1 minute.

Stir in the remaining ingredients and close the lid.

Select MEAT/STEW and cook for 30 minutes. Serve warm.

Pork Meatballs in an Apple Juice Sauce

(Prep + Cook Time: 30 minutes / Servings: 8)

Ingredients:

2 ½ pounds ground Pork
¼ cup Tamari Sauce
3 Garlic Cloves, minced
½ tbsp dried Thyme
½ cup diced Onions
2 tsp Honey
¼ cup Apple Juice
1 ½ cups Water
1 cup Breadcrumbs
Salt and Pepper, to taste

Directions:

Whisk together the honey, tamari, apple juice, water, and thyme in the Crock Pot Express.

Season with salt and pepper.

Choose the MEAT/STEW mode and cook for 10 minutes.

Meanwhile, combine all the remaining ingredients in a bowl.

Shape meatballs out of the mixture.

Release the pressure naturally and drop the meatballs into the sauce.

Close the lid and cook on POULTRY for 15 minutes.

Pork Steaks with Apple and Prunes

(Prep + Cook Time: 30 minutes / Servings: 4)

Ingredients:

4 Pork Steaks
¼ cup Milk
8 Prunes, pitted
½ cup White Wine
2 Apples, peeled and sliced
¼ cup Heavy Cream
1 tbsp Fruit Jelly
½ tsp ground Ginger
Salt and Pepper, to taste

Directions:

Place all of the ingredients, except the jelly, in your Crock Pot Express.

Stir to combine well and season with salt and pepper.

Close the lid and cook on MEAT/STEW for 15 minutes.

Wait 5 minutres before stirring in the jelly.

Pork Sausage with Bell Peppers and Sweet Onions

(Prep + Cook Time: 25 minutes / Servings: 8)

Ingredients:

8 Pork Sausages
2 large Sweet Onions, sliced
4 Bell Peppers, cut into strips
1 tbsp Olive Oil
½ cup Beef Broth
¼ cup White Wine
1 tsp minced Garlic

Directions:

Set your Crock Pot Express to BROWN/SAUTÉ and brown the sausages in it. Transfer to a plate and discard the liquid.

Heat the oil and add the onions and peppers.

Cook for 5 minutes. Add garlic and sausages. Pour over the broth and wine.

Close the lid and cook on SOUP for 10 minutes.

Sweet Ham with Pineapples

(Prep + Cook Time: 30 minutes / Servings: 8)

Ingredients:

3 pounds cooked Ham, chopped
¼ cup Maple Syrup
1 Onion, sliced
14 ounces chopped, canned Pineapple
2 tbsp Brown Sugar
½ cup Apple Butter
¼ tsp Ginger Powder
¼ tsp Cinnamon
¼ tsp Nutmeg
1 tbsp Balsamic Vinegar
Pinch of Salt
½ tsp Pepper

Directions:

Place the ham and onions in your Crock Pot Express.

In a bowl, whisk together the remaining ingredients and pour the mixture over. Stir in the pineapples and close the lid. Cook on RICE/RISOTTO for 18 minutes.

Release the pressure naturally.

Rosemary Dijon Apple Pork

(Prep + Cook Time: 60 minutes / Servings: 6)

Ingredients:

3 ½ pounds Pork Roast
2 Apples, peeled and slices
3 tbsp Dijon Mustard
1 tbsp dried Rosemary
½ cup White Wine
1 tbsp minced Garlic
1 tbsp Oil
Salt and Pepper, to taste

Directions:

Brush the mustard over the pork.

Heat the oil in your Crock Pot Express on BROWN/SAUTÉ and sear the pork on all sides. Add apples and stir in the remaining ingredients.

Select MEAT/STEW, close the lid and cook for 40 minutes.

Release the pressure naturally. The internal temperature should be at least 150 degrees F.

Smothered Cinnamon BBQ Ribs

(Prep + Cook Time: 85 minutes / Servings: 4)

Ingredients:

3 pounds Pork Ribs
½ cup Apple Jelly
1 cup Barbecue Sauce

1 Onion, diced
2 tbsp ground Cloves
½ cup Water
1 tbsp Brown Sugar
1 tsp Worcestershire Sauce
1 tsp ground Cinnamon

Directions:

Whisk together all the ingredients in your Crock Pot Express.

Place the ribs inside and close the lid.

Set the cooker to MEAT/STEW and cook for 60 minutes.

Release the pressure naturally.

Pork Ribs and Pearl Onions Under Pressure

(Prep + Cook Time: 35 minutes / Servings: 4)

Ingredients:

1 pound Pork Ribs
1 ¼ cups Pearl Onions
1 ½ cups Tomato Sauce
1 tbsp minced Garlic
½ tsp Pepper
¾ tsp Salt
1 ½ cups Water

Directions:

Combine all the ingredients in the Crock Pot Express.

Close the lid and set it to MEAT/STEW.

Cook for 30 minutes.

Release the pressure naturally.

Serve hot.

Pork Belly in a Soy Sauce and Star Anise Sauce

(Prep + Cook Time: 40 minutes / Servings: 6)

Ingredients:

1 ½ pounds Pork Belly, sliced
½ cup chopped Sweet Onion
5 Garlic Cloves, sliced
1/3 cup Soy Sauce
¼ cup cooking Wine
1 tsp grated Ginger
½ tsp ground Star Anise
1 tsp Sugar
2 ¼ cup Water

Directions:

Set your Crock Pot Express to BROWN/SAUTÉ and sear it for a few minutes on all sides.

Whisk the remaining ingredients in a bowl and pour the mixture over the pork belly.

Close the lid, select MEAT/STEW and cook for 25 minutes.

Release the pressure naturally.

Barbecue Pork Butt

(Prep + Cook Time: 55 minutes / Servings: 4)

Ingredients:

2 ¼ pounds Pork Butt
¼ tsp Garlic Powder
¼ tsp Pepper
1 cup Barbecue Sauce
¼ tsp Cumin Powder
½ tsp Onion Powder
1 ½ cup Beef Broth

Directions:

Coat your Crock Pot Express with cooking oil and set it to BROWN/SAUTÉ.

Combine the barbecue sauce and all of the spices. Brush this mixture over the pork. Place the pork in the Express Crock and sear on all sides.

Pour the beef broth around the meat. Close the lid and cook for 40 minutes on MEAT/STEW. Press STOP and wait 3-4 minutes before releasing the pressure naturally.

Applesauce and Beer Pulled Pork

(Prep + Cook Time: 70 minutes / Servings: 12)

Ingredients:

3 pounds Pork
1 cup Applesauce
12 ounces Beer
1 Sweet Onion, diced
1 tbsp Orange Marmalade
2 tbsp Brown Sugar
½ tsp Onion Powder
½ tsp Pepper
Pinch of Salt

Directions:

Place the pork in the Crock Pot Express.

Combine the applesauce, beer, onion, brown sugar, pepper, salt, and onion powder in a bowl. Pour this mixture over the pork. Close the lid and set your cooker to MEAT/STEW.

Cook for 60 minutes. Press STOP and release the pressure naturally. Shred the pork with 2 forks inside the cooker.

Stir in the orange marmalade and set it back to MEAT/STEW. Cook for 2 more minutes.

Pork with Rutabaga and Granny Smith Apples

(Prep + Cook Time: 40 minutes / Servings: 4)

Ingredients:

1 pound Pork Loin, cut into cubes
1 Onion, diced
2 Rutabagas, peeled and diced
1 cup Chicken Broth
½ cup White Wine
2 Granny Smith Apples, peeled and diced
½ cup sliced Leeks
1 tbsp Vegetable Oil
1 Celery Stalk, diced
2 tbsp dried Parsley
¼ tsp Thyme
½ tsp Cumin
¼ tsp Lemon Zest
Salt and Pepper, to taste

Directions:

Season the pork with salt and pepper. Heat the oil in your Crock Pot Express on BROWN/SAUTÉ.

Add pork and cook for a few minutes, until browned.

Add the onions and cook for 2 more minutes. Stir in the remaining ingredients, except the apples. Close the lid and cook for 15 minutes on MEAT/STEW.

Press STOP and release the pressure naturally. Stir in the apples, close the lid again, and cook on MEAT/STEW for another 5 minutes.

Spicy Ground Pork

(Prep + Cook Time: 55 minutes / Servings: 6)

Ingredients:

2 pounds Ground Pork
1 Onion, diced
1 can diced Tomatoes

1 can Peas
5 Garlic Cloves, crushed
3 tbsp Butter
1 Serrano Pepper, chopped
2/3 cup Beef Broth
1 tsp ground Ginger
2 tsp ground Coriander
1 tsp Salt
¾ tsp Cumin
¼ tsp Cayenne Pepper
½ tsp Turmeric
½ tsp Black Pepper

Directions:

Set your Crock Pot Express to BROWN/SAUTÉ and melt the butter in it.

Add onions and cook for 3 minutes.

Add the spices and garlic and cook for 2 more minutes.

Add pork and cook until browned.

Add serrano pepper, peas, tomatoes, and beef broth.

Close the lid and cook for 30 minutes on MEAT/STEW.

Brown Sugar Pork

(Prep + Cook Time: 50 minutes / Servings: 6-8)

Ingredients:

3 pounds Pork Roast, cut into cubes
1 ¼ cups Brown Sugar
1 Yellow Onion, chopped
2 tbsp Soy Sauce
1 tsp minced Garlic Clove
3 tbsp Butter
½ cup Lemon Juice
2/3 cup Beef Broth
Salt and Pepper, to taste

Directions:

Set your Crock Pot Express to BROWN/SAUTÉ and melt the butter in it. Add onions and garlic and cook for 2 minutes.

Add the pork and cook for 2 more minutes.

Stir in the lemon juice and beef broth and close the lid.

Cook for 30 minutes on MEAT/STEW mode.

Allow the pressure to release naturally.

Stir in the brown sugar and soy sauce and season with salt and pepper. Cook for 5 more minutes.

Gourmet Bacon, Potato, and Endive Casserole

(Prep + Cook Time: 30 minutes / Servings: 4)

Ingredients:

½ pound Smoked Bacon, chopped
½ cup sliced Carrots
2 cups Water
1 cup Chicken Stock
¾ cup Half and Half
4 Golden Potatoes, peeled and chopped
4 Endives, halved lengthwise
Salt and Pepper, to taste

Directions:

Set your Crock Pot Express to MEAT/STEW and add the bacon. Cook for 2 minutes until slightly crispy.

Add the potatoes, carrots, and chicken stock. Close the lid and cook for 10 minutes. Select STOP and release the pressure naturally.

Add the endive and cook for 5 more minutes.

Press STOP again and release the pressure.

Strain the bacon and veggies and return them back to the Crock Pot Express. Add the half and half and season with salt and pepper. Cook on MEAT/STEW for 3 more minutes.

Pork Sausage with Cauliflower and Tater Tots

(Prep + Cook Time: 20 minutes / Servings: 4)

Ingredients:

1 pound Pork Sausage, sliced
1 pound Tater Tots
1 pound Cauliflower Florets, frozen and thawed
10 ounces canned Mushroom Soup
10 ounces canned Cauliflower Soup
10 ounces Evaporated Milk
Salt and Pepper, to taste

Directions:

Place 1/3 of the sausage slices in your Crocl Pot Express.

In a bowl, whisk together the soups and milk. Pour some of the mixture over the sausages.

Top the sausage slices with 1/3 of the cauliflower florets followed by 1/3 of the tater tots.

Pour some of the soup mixture again. Repeat the layers until you use all of the ingredients.

Close the lid and cook on MEAT/STEW for 7 minutes.

Release the pressure naturally.

Pork Chops in Merlot

(Prep + Cook Time: 30 minutes / Servings: 4)

Ingredients:

4 Pork Chops
3 Carrots, chopped
1 Tomato, chopped
1 Onion, chopped
2 Garlic Cloves, minced
4 ounces Merlot
1 tsp dried Oregano
2 tbsp Olive Oil

2 tbsp Flour
2 tbsp Water
2 tbsp Tomato Paste
1 Beef Bouillon Cube
¼ tsp Pepper
¼ tsp Salt

Directions:

Set your Crock Pot Express on BROWN/SAUTÉ and heat the oil in it.

Toss the pork chops with the flour, pepper, and salt.

Place in the cooker and cook for a few minutes, until browned on all sides.

Add the carrots, chopped, garlic, and oregano.

Cook for a few minutes more. Stir in the remaining ingredients and close the lid. Choose MEAT/STEW and cook for 25 minutes.

Do a natural pressure release and serve.

Dinner Pork Roast

(Prep + Cook Time: 45 minutes / Servings: 8)

Ingredients:

3 pound Sirloin Pork Roast
1 tbsp Honey
1 tsp Chili Powder
1 tbsp Rosemary
1 tbsp Olive Oil
1 ¼ cups Water
2 tbsp Lemon Juice

Directions:

Combine the spices and rub them into the pork.

Heat the oil in your Crock Pot Express on BROWN/SAUTÉ and sear the pork on all sides.

Stir in the remaining ingredients and close the lid.

Select MEAT/STEW, cook for 30 minutes and allow for a natural pressure release.

Pork Chops and Mushrooms in a Tomato Sauce

(Prep + Cook Time: 35minutes / Servings: 4)

Ingredients:

4 large Bone-In Pork Chops
1 cup Tomato Sauce
1 ½ cups sliced White Button Mushrooms
1 Onion, chopped
1 tsp minced Garlic
½ cup Water
1 tbsp Oil
Salt and Pepper, to taste

Directions:

Heat the oil in your Crock Pot Express on BROWN/SAUTÉ.

Add garlic and onion and cook for 2 minutes.

Add pork and cook until browned on all sides.

Stir in the remaining ingredients and close the lid.

Cook on MEAT/STEW for 20 minutes.

Allow the pressure to release naturally.

Apple and Cherry Pork Tenderloin

(Prep + Cook Time: 55 minutes / Servings: 4)

Ingredients:

1 1/3 pounds Pork Tenderloin
1/3 cup chopped Celery
2 cups peeled and chopped Apples
2/3 cup pitted Cherries
½ cup Apple Juice
¼ cup Water
1/3 cup chopped Onion
Salt and Pepper, to taste

Directions:

Combine all of the ingredients in your Crock Pot Express.

Close the lid and select the MEAT/STEW mode. Cook for 40 minutes. Wait 5 minutes before releasing the pressure naturally.

Braised Chili Pork Chops

(Prep + Cook Time: 30 minutes / Servings: 4)

Ingredients:

4 Pork Chops
1 Onion, chopped
2 tbsp Chili Powder
14 ounces canned Tomatoes with Green Chilies
1 Garlic Clove, minced
½ cup Beer
1 tsp Oil

Directions:

Heat the oil in your Crock Pot Express on BROWN/SAUTÉ.

Add onion, garlic, and chili powder and cook for 2 minutes.

Add the pork chops and cook until browned on all sides.

Stir in the tomatoes and beer. Season with salt and pepper.

Close the lid and cook on BEANS/CHILI for 20 minutes.

Release the pressure naturally and serve.

Ham and Bacon with Veggies

(Prep + Cook Time: 20 minutes / Servings: 4)

Ingredients:

8 Bacon Slices, chopped
8 ounces cooked Ham, diced
3 Potatoes, diced
1 Onion, diced
1 Zucchini, grated

2 Carrots, grated
½ pound Brussel Sprouts, quartered
Salt and Pepper, to taste

Directions:

Cook the bacon in your Crock Pot Express on BROWN/SAUTÉ for a few minutes, until crispy.

Add onion and cook for 2 more minutes.

Stir in the remaining ingredients.

Season with salt and pepper and close the lid.

Cook on BEANS/CHILI for 10 minutes.

Press STOP and release the pressure naturally.

Beef

Beef Cabbage Rolls in a Tomato Sauce

(Prep + Cook Time: 55 minutes / Servings: 6)

Ingredients:

10 Cabbage Leaves, blanched
1 ½ pounds ground Beef
2 cups Rice, cooked
22 ounces canned diced Tomatoes
1 tbsp minced Garlic
15 ounces Tomato Sauce
1 Onion, chopped
½ tsp Cayenne Pepper
Salt and Pepper, to taste

Directions:

In a bowl, combine the beef, rice, cayenne pepper, garlic, tomato sauce, and onions.

Divide this mixture between the cabbage rolls and roll them up. Arrange the rolls in the Crock Pot Express and pour the diced tomatoes over.

Close the lid and cook on MEAT/STEW for 40 minutes.

Press STOP and wait 5 minutes before releasing the pressure naturally.

Chuck Roast with Potatoes

(Prep + Cook Time: 4 hours / Servings: 6)

Ingredients:

2 ½ pounds Chuck Roast
1 pound Red Potatoes, chopped
2 Carrots, chopped
½ cup chopped Parsnips
1 cup sliced Onions
1/3 cup Red Wine

½ Celery Stalk, sliced
1 tbsp Rosemary
1 tsp Thyme
½ tsp Pepper
2 tbsp Tomato Paste
1 tbsp minced Garlic
2/3 cup Beef Broth

Directions:

Coat the Crock Pot Express with cooking spray and set it to BROWN/SAUTÉ.

Combine the thyme, rosemary, salt, and pepper and rub the mixture onto the meat. Sear the beef on all sides. Add the remaining ingredients and close the lid.

Cook for 4 hours on SLOW COOK. Allow the pressure to release naturally.

Beef Ribs with Button Mushrooms

(Prep + Cook Time: 30 minutes / Servings: 4)

Ingredients:

2 pounds Beef Ribs
2 cups quartered White Button Mushrooms
1 Onion, chopped
¼ cup Ketchup
2 ½ cups Veggie Stock
1 cup chopped Carrots
¼ cup Olive Oil
1 tsp minced Garlic
Salt and Pepper, to taste

Directions:

Heat the oil in your Crock Pot Express on BROWN/SAUTÉ. Season the ribs with salt and pepper and brown them on all sides. Set aside.

Add the onion, garlic, carrots, and mushrooms and cook for 5 minutes. Add the ribs back to the cooker and stir in the remaining ingredients. Close the lid and cook for 35 minutes on MEAT/STEW.

Allow the pressure to release naturally.

Beef Medley with Blue Cheese and Cabbage

(Prep + Cook Time: 50 minutes / Servings: 6)

Ingredients:

1 pound Sirloin Steak, cut into cubes
6 ounces Blue Cheese, crumbled
½ Cabbage, diced
1 cup chopped Parsnip
2 Bell Peppers, chopped
½ cup Beef Broth
2 cups canned Tomatoes, undrained
1 Onion, diced
1 tsp minced Garlic
Salt and Pepper, to taste

Directions:

Coat the Crock Pot Express with cooking spray and brown the steak on BROWN/ SAUTÉ.

Add the remaining ingredients, except the cheese.

Close the lid and cook for 40 minutes on MEAT/STEW.

Release the pressure naturally. Top with blue cheese and serve.

Basil and Thyme Pot Roast

(Prep + Cook Time: 55 minutes / Servings: 6)

Ingredients:

2 pounds Beef Roast, cubed
2 Yams, chopped
4 Garlic Cloves, minced
2 Bell Peppers, chopped
1 Red Onion, chopped
½ pounds Baby Carrots
1 ½ cups Bone Broth
½ tbsp dried Basil
2 tsp dried Thyme

1 cup Tomato Paste
2 tsp Oil
Salt and Pepper, to taste

Directions:

Season the meat with salt and pepper. Heat the oil in the cooker on BROWN/ SAUTÉ. Add the meat and cook until browned. Stir in the remaining ingredients.

Close the lid and cook for 40 minutes on MEAT/STEW.

Wait 5 minutes before doing a quick pressure release.

Steak and Veggies in an Ale Sauce

(Prep + Cook Time: 50 minutes / Servings: 6-8)

Ingredients:

2 pounds Beef Steak, cut into 6 or 8 equal pieces
1 Sweet Onion, chopped
1 cup chopped Celery
1 pound Sweet Potatoes, chopped
2 Carrots, chopped
3 Garlic Cloves, minced
2 Bell Peppers, chopped
1 ½ cups Tomato Puree
½ cup Ale
1 Chicken Bouillon Cube
Salt and Pepper, to taste

Directions:

Coat the Crock Pot Express with cooking spray and brown the steaks on all sides on BROWN/SAUTÉ. Set aside.

Place the veggies in the Crock Pot Express and top with the steak.

Whisk together the bouillon cube, ale, and tomato puree.

Pour this mixture over the steaks. Season with salt and pepper and close the lid.

Cook for 30 minutes on BEANS/CHILI on high pressure.

Release the pressure naturally.

Worcestershire Beef Brisket

(Prep + Cook Time: 60 minutes / Servings: 4)

Ingredients:

1 ½ pounds Beef Brisket
1 tbsp Worcestershire Sauce
1 tsp Onion Powder
1 tbsp Ketchup
1 tsp minced Garlic
2 cups Beef Stock
1 tbsp Brown Sugar
2 tbsp Apple Cider Vinegar
1 tsp Cayenne Pepper
¼ tsp Pepper
½ tsp Salt

Directions:

Place the beef in your Crock Pot Express. Whisk together the remaining ingredients in a bowl.

Pour this mixture over the beef. Close the lid and choose the BEANS/CHILI mode. Cook for 40 minutes on high pressure. Release the pressure naturally.

Beef in a Creamy Sour Sauce

(Prep + Cook Time: 35 minutes / Servings: 6)

Ingredients:

1 ½ pounds Beef Roast, cubed
1 cup diced Onion
1 can Cream of Mushroom Soup
1 ½ cups Sour Cream
½ tbsp Cumin
½ tbsp Coriander
1 tbsp minced Garlic
1 tbsp Butter
½ tsp Chili Powder
Salt and Pepper, to taste

Directions:

Melt the butter in your Crock Pot Express on BROWN/SAUTÉ and cook the onion until soft.

Add garlic and cook for one more minute.

Add the beef and cook until browned.

Combine the remaining ingredients in a bowl and pour this mixture over the beef.

Close the lid and cook for 20 minutes on MEAT/STEW.

Allow the pressure to release naturally.

Ground Beef, Leek, and Sauerkraut

(Prep + Cook Time: 50 minutes / Servings: 6)

Ingredients:

1 ½ pounds Ground Beef
10 ounces canned Tomato Soup
3 cups Sauerkraut
1 cup sliced Leeks
1 tbsp Butter
1 tsp Mustard Powder
Salt and Pepper, to taste

Directions:

Melt the butter in the Crock Pot Express on BROWN/SAUTÉ.

Add the leeks and cook for a few minutes.

Add beef and cook until browned.

Stir in the sauerkraut and mustard powder and season with some salt and pepper.

Close the lid and cook for 15 minutes on BEANS/CHILI mode.

Allow the pressure to release naturally.

Corned Beef in a Celery Sauce

(Prep + Cook Time: 50 minutes / Servings: 4-6)

Ingredients:

1 ½ pounds Corned Beef Brisket
1 ½ cups Cream of Celery Soup
1 tsp minced Garlic
1 Onion, diced
2 Tomatoes, diced
2 tsp Oil
Salt and Pepper, to taste

Directions:

Season the beef with salt and pepper.

Heat the oil in the Crock Pot Express on BROWN/SAUTÉ.

Add onions and cook for 2 minutes.

Add garlic and cook for one more minute.

Add beef and sear on all sides.

Pour the celery soup over.

Close the lid and cook for 40 minutes on MEAT/STEW.

Allow the pressure to release naturally.

Beef Sausage and Red Cabbage Casserole

(Prep + Cook Time: 30 minutes / Servings: 4)

Ingredients:

1 pound Beef Sausage, crumbled
1 pound Red Cabbage, shredded
1 ½ cups Tomato Puree
1 cup Rice
1 tbsp Cider Vinegar
½ tsp Fennel Seeds
1/3 cup chopped Scallions
Salt and Pepper, to taste

Directions:

Season the cabbage with the fennel in a bowl.

Place half of this mixture in the Crock Pot Express.

Combine the sausage, rice, and scallions in another bowl.

Place half of this mixture over the cabbage. Repeat the layers. Whisk together the vinegar, tomato puree, and salt and pepper.

Pour this mixture over the sausage. Close the lid and cook on MEAT/STEW for 15 minutes. Allow the pressure to release naturally.

Drunken Beef and Mushrooms

(Prep + Cook Time: 60 minutes / Servings: 6)

Ingredients:

2 pounds Beef Roast
1 pound White Button Mushrooms, quartered
2 tbsp Tomato Paste
1 Onion, chopped
1 tsp minced Garlic
1 cup Red Wine
1 cup Beef Broth
1 Tomato, diced
1 tbsp Olive Oil
¼ tsp Pepper
¼ tsp Salt

Directions:

Heat the oil in your Crock Pot Express on BROWN/SAUTÉ.

Season the beef with salt and pepper.

Sauté the onion for 2 minutes. Add beef and sear on all sides. Whisk together the remaining ingredients in a bowl.

Pour over the meat. Close the lid and cook for 40 minutes on MEAT/STEW.

Release the pressure naturally.

Dark Beer and Dijon Braised Steak

(Prep + Cook Time: 40 minutes / Servings: 4)

Ingredients:

4 Beef Steaks
12 ounces Dark Beer
2 tbsp Dijon Mustard
2 Carrots, chopped
1 tbsp Tomato Paste
1 Onion, chopped
1 tsp Paprika
2 tbsp Flour
1 cup Beef Broth
Salt and Pepper, to taste

Directions:

Brush the meat with the mustard and sprinkle with paprika, salt, and pepper.

Coat the Crock Pot Express with cooking spray and sear the steak on BROWN/ SAUTÉ. Transfer the steaks to a plate. Pour ¼ cup beer and scrape the bottom of the cooker.

Whisk in the tomato paste and flour. Gradually stir in the remaining ingredients. Return the steak to the cooker and close the lid. Cook for 15 minutes on BEANS/ CHILI on HIGH pressure.

Release the pressure naturally and serve.

Tender Onion Beef Roast

(Prep + Cook Time: 55 minutes / Servings: 8)

Ingredients:

3 pounds Beef Roast
2 Large Sweet Onions, sliced
1 envelope Onion Mix
1 cup Beef Broth
1 cup Tomato Juice
1 tsp minced Garlic
1 tbsp Worcestershire Sauce

1 tbsp Olive Oil
Salt and Pepper, to taste

Directions:

Heat the oil in your Crock Pot Express on BROWN/SAUTÉ.

Season the beef with salt and pepper and sear it on all sides. Transfer to a plate.

Add the onions and cook for 3 minutes. Add garlic and cook for 1 more minutes. Add beef and stir in the remaining ingredients.

Close the lid and cook for 40 minutes on BEANS/CHILI mode. Release the pressure naturally.

Beef Enchilada Casserole

(Prep + Cook Time: 35 minutes / Servings: 8)

Ingredients:

2 pounds ground Beef
12 ounces Enchilada Sauce
10 ounces canned Mushroom Soup
10 ounces canned Cheddar Cheese Soup
10 ounces canned Celery Soup
2 Shallots, diced
1 Jalapeno, chopped
2 cups refried Beans
½ tsp Chili Powder
½ tsp Cumin
8 ounces Tortilla Chips

Directions:

Coat the Crock Pot Express with cooking spray, add shallots and beef and cook on BEANS/CHILI for 5 minutes.

Stir in the jalapeno, spices, soups, beans, and enchilada sauce.

Close the lid and cook for 5 minutes.

Allow the pressure to release naturally and stir in the chips.

Close the lid and cook for 15 more minutes.

Spicy Shredded Beef

(Prep + Cook Time: 3 hours / Servings: 8)

Ingredients:

3 pounds Beef Roast
½ cup Ketchup
½ cup Red Wine
1 cup Water
2 tsp Soy Sauce
1 tbsp Brown Sugar
1 tbsp Balsamic Vinegar
2 tbsp minced Onions
2 tsp Mustard Powder
1 tsp Chili Powder
1 tsp minced Garlic
¼ tsp Nutmeg
½ tsp Cinnamon
1 tsp Pepper
¼ tsp Salt
¼ tsp Ginger

Directions:

Place the beef in your Crock Pot Express.

Whisk together the remaining ingredients in a bowl.

Pour this mixture over the beef.

Close the lid and cook for 3 hours on SLOW COOK mode.

Teriyaki and Peach Pulled Beef

(Prep + Cook Time: 5 hours / Servings: 10)

Ingredients:

4 pounds Beef Roast
½ cup Teriyaki Sauce
½ cup Peach Preserves
½ cup Ketchup

¼ cup Apple Cider Vinegar
¼ cup Brown Sugar
1 tsp Dijon Mustard
1 ½ cups Water
1 Onion, sliced
½ tsp Pepper
Pinch of Salt

Directions:

Cut the meat in 4 equal pieces and stir in the remaining ingredients.

Cover and let marinate for 50-60 minutes.

Place the beef along with the marinade in the Crock Pot Express.

Close the lid and cook on SLOW COOK mode for 4 hours.

Shred the beef with two forks.

Steaks with Onion and Gravy

(Prep + Cook Time: 30 minutes / Servings: 4)

Ingredients:

4 Round Steaks
2 Onions, sliced
1 cup Beef Broth
1 tsp minced Garlic
1 tbsp dried Parsley
½ tsp Rosemary
1 tbsp Oil
½ tsp Red Pepper Flakes
¼ cup Half and Half
2 tbsp Flour
¼ tsp Salt
¼ tsp Pepper

Directions:

Heat the oil in your Crock Pot Express on BROWN/SAUTÉ.

Brown the steaks on all sides and transfer to a plate.

Sauté the onions and garlic for 2 minutes.

Return the steaks to the multi-cooker.

Stir in the salt, pepper, pepper flakes, rosemary, parsley, and broth.

Close the lid and cook for 20 minutes on BEANS/CHILI mode.

Stir in the flour and half and half.

Cook for 3 more minutes, until thickened.

Pressure Cooked Beef Burritos

(Prep + Cook Time: 60 minutes / Servings: 6)

Ingredients:

2 pounds Beef Brisket
6 Burrito Shells
10 ounces Enchilada Sauce
1 Sweet Onion, diced
1 Bell Pepper, diced
½ tsp Chili Powder
½ tsp Cumin
¼ cup Water

Directions:

Combine all of the ingredients, except the burrito shells, in the Crock Pot Express.

Close the lid and cook on MEAT/STEW for 40 minutes.

Shred the meat inside the cooker.

Divide between the burrito shells.

Dijon Rump Roast with Potatoes

(Prep + Cook Time: 2 hours / Servings: 6)

Ingredients:

3-pound Rump Roast
6 medium Red Potatoes, quartered
1 Onion, diced

1 Celery Stalk, chopped
1 ½ tbsp Dijon Mustard
2 cups Beef Broth
1 tbsp Butter
2 Garlic Cloves, minced
Salt and Pepper, to taste

Directions:

Heat the oil in your Crock Pot Express on BROWN/SAUTÉ.

Cook the onion and celery for a few minutes.

Brush the mustard over the beef and season with some salt and pepper. Sear on all sides. Stir in the remaining ingredients.

Close the lid and press SLOW COOK mode. Cook for 2 hours.

Sloppy Joes

(Prep + Cook Time: 50 minutes / Servings: 8)

Ingredients:

1 ½ pounds Ground Beef
2 Tomatoes, diced
8 Kaiser Rolls
1/3 cup Barley
1 tsp Chili Powder
3 tsp Canola Oil
¼ cup Worcestershire Sauce
¼ cup Tomato Ketchup
2 tbsp Brown Sugar
1 cup chopped Scallions
½ tbsp Cayenne Pepper
3 cups Water

Directions:

Combine all of the ingredients, except the rolls, in your Crock Pot Express.

Set it to BEANS/CHILI and cook for 25 minutes on HIGH pressure. Allow the pressure to release naturally.

Divide the mixture between the rolls.

Sweet Balsamic Beef

(Prep + Cook Time: 55 minutes / Servings: 8)

Ingredients:

3 pounds Chuck Steak, sliced
1 cup Maple Syrup
½ cup Balsamic Vinegar
1 cup Bone Broth
1 tsp minced Garlic
1 tsp Salt
2 tbsp Olive Oil
1 tsp ground Ginger

Directions:

Heat the oil in your Crock Pot Express on BROWN/SAUTÉ.

Season the beef with salt and ginger. Brown on all sides in the muti-cooker. Stir in the remaining ingredients.

Close the lid and cook for 45 minutes on MEAT/STEW mode. Release the pressure naturally and serve.

Marinated Flank Steak

(Prep + Cook Time: 80 minutes / Servings: 4)

Ingredients:

2 pounds Flank Steak
½ cup Beef Broth
1 Onion, diced
2 tbsp Potato Starch
1 Carrot, chopped

Marinade:

2 tbsp Fish Sauce
½ tsp Cajun Seasoning
2 tsp minced Garlic
½ cup Soy Sauce
1 tbsp Sesame Oil

Directions:

Combine the marinade ingredients in a bowl. Add the beef and let marinate for 30 minutes. Coat the multi-cooker with cooking spray.

Add onions and carrots and cook until soft on BROWN/SAUTÉ. Add the beef along with the marinade.

Whisk in the broth and starch. Close the lid and cook for 40 minutes MEAT/ STEW mode. Release the pressure naturally.

Tomato Meatballs

(Prep + Cook Time: 30 minutes / Servings: 4)

Ingredients:

1 pound ground Beef
½ cup Breadcrumbs
½ Onion, diced
1 tsp minced Garlic
1 Egg
1 tsp dried Parsley
1 tsp dried Thyme
¼ tsp Salt
¼ tsp Pepper
1 cup Tomato Juice
1 cup canned Diced Tomatoes
1 tbsp Brown Sugar
¼ tsp Garlic Powder
¼ tsp Oregano

Directions:

Combine all ingredients, except the tomatoes and tomato juice, the suger, garlic powder and oregano, in a bowl.

Shape the mixture into meatballs. Coat the Crock Pot Express with cooking spray.

Cook the meatballs until brown on BEANS/CHILI mode.

Stir in the remaining ingredients. Close the lid and cook for 20 minutes. Release the pressure naturally.

Bourbon and Apricot Meatloaf

(Prep + Cook Time: 30 minutes / Servings: 4)

Ingredients:

1 ½ cups Water
Meatloaf:
1 pound ground Beef
1 Egg White
2/3 cup Breadcrumbs
2 tbsp Ketchup
2/3 cup diced Onion
½ tsp Basil
1 tsp minced Garlic

Glaze:

1 cup Apricot Jam
½ cup Bourbon
½ cup Barbecue Sauce
¼ cup Honey
¼ cup Water
1 tbsp Hot Sauce

Directions:

Combine all of the meatloaf ingredients in a bowl. Shape into a meatloaf and place on a greased pan that can fit in your Express Crock Pot.

Whisk the glaze ingredients in a bowl. Brush this mixture over the meatloaf. Set your Multi-Cooker to MEAT/STEW and pour the water inside.

Place the baking dish in the Crock Pot Express and close the lid. Cook for 50 minutes. Allow the pressure to release naturally.

Herbed Beef Cubes

(Prep + Cook Time: 35 minutes / Servings: 6)

Ingredients:

3 pounds Beef Roast, cut into cubes
2 tsp Thyme

2 tsp Oregano
2 tsp Parsley
2 tsp Rosemary
2 minced Garlic Cloves
2 tbsp Olive Oil
3 tbsp Flour
½ tsp salt
¼ tsp Pepper
1 ½ cups Beef Broth

Directions:

Heat the oil in your Crock Pot Express on BROWN/SAUTÉ.

Season the beef with the salt and pepper and toss with flour.

Cook until browned on all sides.

Stir in the remaining ingredients and close the lid.

Cook for 30 minutes on MEAT/STEW mode.

Press STOP and release the pressure naturally.

Simple Cheesy Meatballs

(Prep + Cook Time: 30 minutes / Servings: 4)

Ingredients:

1 pound ground Beef
½ cup diced Onion
1 Egg
½ tsp Garlic Powder
½ cup crumbled Feta Cheese
1 tbsp mixed dried Herbs
½ cup Breadcrumbs
¼ tsp Pepper
1 cup canned Cream of Mushroom Soup
¼ cup Water
½ cup grated Cheddar Cheese

Directions:

In a bowl, combine the first 8 ingredients. Shape into meatballs.

Coat the Crock Pot Express with cooking spray on BROWN/SAUTÉ.

Add the meatballs and brown on all sides.

Pour the water and soup over, close the lid, and cook for 15 minutes on BEANS/ CHILI mode.

After that, stir in the cheddar cheese.

Cook for additional 3 minutes.

Coconut Beef with Plantains

(Prep + Cook Time: 50 minutes / Servings: 4)

Ingredients:

1 ¾ pound Beef Roast, cubed
1 cup Coconut Milk
2 Onions, sliced
1 Plantain, chopped
1 tbsp Coconut Oil
1 tsp ground Ginger
1 tsp Garlic Powder
½ tsp Turmeric

Directions:

Season the beef with all of the spices.

Melt the coconut oil in your Crock Pot Express.

Add the beef and cook until brown on BEANS/CHILI.

Add onions and cook for 3 more minutes.

Pour the coconut milk over and close the lid. Cook for 30 minutes.

Stir in the plantain.

Cook for another 5-7 minutes.

Beef Hot Pot

(Prep + Cook Time: 40 minutes / Servings: 4)

Ingredients:

1 ½ pounds Beef Stew Meat, cubed
2 Carrots, chopped
2 Celery Stalks, chopped
4 Potatoes, chopped
1 Onion, chopped
2 cups Water
2 tbsp Red Wine
2 tbsp Olive Oil
4 tbsp Flour
1 tsp Thyme
Salt and Pepper, to taste

Directions:

Toss the beef cubes with the flour, salt, and pepper. Heat the oil in your Multi-Cooker on BROWN/SAUTÉ

Add the beef and cook until browned. Add onion and cook for 2 minutes. Stir in the remaining ingredients.

Close the lid and cook for 25 minutes on MEAT/STEW. Release the pressure naturally.

Mexican Brisket

(Prep + Cook Time: 55 minutes / Servings: 6)

Ingredients:

2 ½ pounds Beef Brisket
1 tbsp Chili Powder
1 tbsp Tomato Paste
½ cup Salsa
½ cup Beef Broth
1 tbsp Butter
1 Spanish Onion, sliced
2 Garlic Cloves, minced

Directions:

Season the beef with chili powder.

Coat the Crock Pot Express with cooking spray and SAUTÉ the beef until browned on all sides.

Add onion and cook for 2 more minutes.

Stir in the remaining ingredients.

Close the lid and press MEAT/STEW.

Cook on HIGH for 35 minutes.

Snacks & Appetizers

Buttery Beets

(Prep + Cook Time: 30 minutes / Servings: 4)

Ingredients:

1 tbsp Olive Oil
1 pound Beets, peeled and sliced
½ tsp Garlic Salt
4 tbsp Butter, melted
1 tsp dried Basil
1 cup Chicken Broth

Directions:

Combine the beets and broth in your Crock Pot Express. Cook on BEANS/ CHILI for 20 minutes. Drain the liquid and sprinkle the beets with olive oil.

Cook with the lid off for 5 minutes. Sprinkle with garlic salt and basil and cook for 2 more. Serve drizzled with the melted butter.

Corn on the Cob

(Prep + Cook Time: 15 minutes / Servings: 4)

Ingredients:

4 Fresh Corn on the Cob
½ cup Butter
1/3 tsp Spice by choice
¼ tsp Salt
1 ½ cup Water

Directions:

Pour the water in your Crock Pot Express and add the corn inside. Close the lid and cook on BEANS/CHILI for 10 minutes.

Release the pressure naturally. Drain the water and add the spices and butter.

Cook for 1 minute or until the butter is melted and the corn is well coated.

Agave Carrot Sticks

(Prep + Cook Time: 10 minutes / Servings: 4)

Ingredients:

1 pound Carrots, sliced into sticks
½ Stick Butter, melted
2 tbsp Agave Nectar
1 ½ cups Water
½ tsp Cinnamon
Pinch of Salt

Directions:

Place the water and carrot sticks in your Crock Pot Express.

Close the lid and cook on STEAM for 4 minutes.

Release the pressure naturally. Whisk together the remaining ingredients and coat the carrots with this mixture.

Pressure Cooked Eggplant Dip

(Prep + Cook Time: 20 minutes / Servings: 8)

Ingredients:

2 Eggplants, diced
¾ cup Water
¼ cup chopped Cilantro
2 Garlic Cloves
1 ½ tbsp Sesame Paste
2 tbsp Oil
½ tsp Pepper
½ tsp Salt

Directions:

Combine the water and eggplants in your Crock Pot Express.

Close the lid and choose the STEAM cooking mode.

Cook for 10 minutes. Release the pressure naturally and transfer the drained eggplants to a food processor.

Add the remaining ingredients. Process until smooth.

Serve with carrot and celery sticks.

Cheese and Polenta Balls

(Prep + Cook Time: 15 minutes / Servings: 6)

Ingredients:

2 cups Polenta
1 cup chopped Onions
½ cup grated Cheddar Cheese
1 Butter Stick, melted
1 ½ cups Water
3 cups Veggie Stock
½ tsp Salt
¼ tsp Pepper

Directions:

Melt 2 tbsp of the butter in your Crock Pot Express on BROWN/SAUTÉ.

Cook the onion until soft, for a few minutes.

Add the water, veggie stock, polenta, pepper, and salt.

Close the lid and cook for 10 minutes on BEANS/CHILI mode.

Stir in the cheddar and the rest of the butter.

Let cool completely. Make balls out of the mixture.

Chili Peanuts

(Prep + Cook Time: 50 minutes / Servings: 16)

Ingredients:

2 ¼ cup Peanuts
1 tsp Chili Powder
¼ cup Sea Salt
½ tsp Garlic Powder
4 quarts Water

Directions:

Place the water and peanuts in your Crock Pot Express.

Close the lid and cook on MEAT/STEW for 40 minutes.

Select STOP and release the pressure naturally.

Sprinkle with the spices.

Potato Sticks

(Prep + Cook Time: 20 minutes / Servings: 6)

Ingredients:

2 pounds Potatoes, cut into sticks
1 tsp Salt
½ tsp Paprika
¼ tsp Pepper
1 ½ cup Water
1 tbsp Butter, melted

Directions:

Place all ingredients, except the butter, in your Crock Pot Express.

Close the lid and cook for 15 minutes on SOUP.

Release the pressure naturally.

Drain the liquid and drizzle the butter over.

Kale Hummus

(Prep + Cook Time: 25 minutes / Servings: 10)

Ingredients:

2 cups Chickpeas
2 cups chopped Kale
3 tbsp Tahini
1 cup minced Green Onions
4 ½ cups Water
½ tsp Salt

¼ tsp Pepper
2 tbsp Olive Oil

Directions:

Combine the chickpeas and water in your Crock Pot Express.

Close the lid and cook on BEANS/CHILI for 20 minutes. Release the pressure naturally.

Transfer the drained chickpeas to a food processor.

Add the remaining ingredients. Process until smooth and serve.

Ricotta and Cheddar Veggie Appetizer

(Prep + Cook Time: 25 minutes / Servings: 6)

Ingredients:

1 cup grated Cheddar Cheese
½ cup Ricotta Cheese
1 ½ pounds Potatoes, diced
1 cup Broccoli Florets
½ cup chopped Carrots
¾ tsp Paprika
1/3 tsp Cumin Powder
1 ½ cups Water
2 tbsp Oil
1 tsp Salt

Directions:

Combine the water, potatoes, carrots, and broccoli, in your Crock Pot Express.

Close the lid and cook on BEANS/CHILI for 15 minutes.

Drain the veggies and place in a food processor.

Add the remaining ingredients and process until smooth.

Chill until ready to serve.

Appetizer Meatballs

(Prep + Cook Time: 25 minutes / Servings: 8)

Ingredients:

½ pound ground Pork
½ pound ground Beef
½ cup Grape Jelly
1 tbsp Mustard
1 cup diced Onions
2/3 cup Breadcrumbs
1 ½ tbsp Cornstarch
¼ cup Sugar
¼ cup Chili Sauce
Salt and Pepper, to taste
1 ½ cup Water

Directions:

Combine the meat, breadcrumbs, and onion in a large bowl.

Season with salt and pepper. Form small meatballs out of the mixture.

Coat the Crock Pot Express with some cooking spray and cook the meatballs on BEANS/CHILI until slightly browned. Transfer to a plate.

Whisk together the remaining ingredients in the Multi-cooker. Press STOP and add the meatballs.

Close the lid and cook on MEAT/STEW for 20 minutes.

Release the pressure naturally.

Sliced Parsnips with Walnuts

(Prep + Cook Time: 10 minutes / Servings: 4)

Ingredients:

2 pounds Parsnips, peeled and sliced
¼ cup chopped toasted Walnuts
1 tbsp Butter
1 tbsp Champagne Vinegar
1 cup Water

½ tsp Salt
¼ tsp Pepper

Directions:

Melt the butter in your Crock Pot Express on BROWN/SAUTÉ.

Add the parsnip slices and sauté for a few minutes, until tender. Stir in the remaining ingredients.

Close the lid and cook for 5 minutes on STEAM. Release the pressure naturally.

Potato Rounds with Gorgonzola

(Prep + Cook Time: 20 minutes / Servings: 4)

Ingredients:

1 ½ pounds Fingerling Potatoes, peeled and cut into slices
1 cup crumbled Gorgonzola Cheese
4 tbsp Butter
1/3 cup Beef Broth
½ tsp Cayenne Pepper
½ tsp Salt

Directions:

Melt the butter in the Crock Pot Express on BROWN/SAUTÉ.

Add the potato slices, beef broth, salt, and pepper.

Close the lid and cook for 10 minutes.

Serve the potatoes topped with crumbled blue cheese.

Candied Cinnamon Pecans

(Prep + Cook Time: 20 minutes / Servings: 6)

Ingredients:

4 cups Pecans
1 cup Maple Syrup
1 tsp Cinnamon
½ tsp Nutmeg

½ cup Water
¼ tsp Ginger Powder
Pinch of Sea Salt

Directions:

Combine all of the ingredients in your Crock Pot Express.

Close the lid and cook for 10 minutes on SOUP.

Allow the pressure to release naturally.

Mini Beefy Cabbage Rolls

(Prep + Cook Time: 35 minutes / Servings: 15)

Ingredients:

1 Cabbage, leaves separated
1 pound ground Beef
1 Bell Pepper, chopped
1 cup Rice
1 cup Beef Broth
3 cups Water
2 tbsp Lemon Juice
1 Onion, diced
1/3 cup Olive Oil
1 tsp Fennel Seeds
Salt and Pepper, to taste

Directions:

Place 1 cup of water and the cabbage leaves in the Crock Pot Express.

Close the lid and cook on STEAM for 2 minutes.

Release the pressure naturally. Place in an ice bath to cool.

Combine the remaining ingredients except water and broth.

Divide this mixture between the cabbage leaves.

Roll them up and place in the Crock Pot Express.

Pour the water and broth over. Close the lid and cook for 15 minutes on MEAT/ STEW. Allow the pressure to release naturally.

Southern Chicken Dip

(Prep + Cook Time: 30 minutes / Servings: 12)

Ingredients:

1 pound Chicken Breasts, cut into cubes
3 Bacon Slices, chopped
1 cup shredded Cheddar Cheese
½ cup Sour Cream
½ cup Salsa
1 Onion, diced
¼ cup Ketchup
½ cup minced Cilantro
2 tbsp Olive Oil
½ cup Chicken Broth
3 Garlic Cloves
½ tsp Onion Powder
1 tbsp Flour
½ tsp Cumin
½ tsp Cayenne Pepper
1 tsp Chili Powder

Directions:

Heat the oil and cook the bacon in your Crock Pot Express on BROWN/SAUTÉ.

Add onions, cilantro, and garlic. Cook for 3 minutes

Stir in the chicken, salsa, broth, and spices.

Close the lid and cook for 15 minutes.

Release the pressure naturally.

Whisk in the flour and cook for a few more minutes, until thickened.

Transfer to a food processor.

Add the cheddar and sour cream.

Pulse until smooth.

Serve with crackers and enjoy!

Minty Grape Leaves

(Prep + Cook Time: 40 minutes / Servings: 12)

Ingredients:

16 ounces jarred Grape Leaves
1 cup Brown Rice
½ cup Mint
¼ cup Parsley
2 cups Veggie Broth
Juice from 3 Lemons
½ tsp Lemon Zest
1 tsp minced Garlic
1 tsp Salt
4 Scallions, diced

Directions:

Coat the Crock Pot Express with cooking spray.

Add scallions, mint, and parsley. Press START/STOP, then BROWN/SAUTÉ and cook for 2 minutes.

Stir in the rice, broth, zest, and salt. Close the lid and cook on MEAT/STEW for 10 minutes. Release the pressure naturally and transfer to a bowl.

Divide the mixture between the grape leaves. Roll them up and arrange in a steamer basket. Drizzle the lemon juice over and cover with foil.

Close the lid and cook for 10 more minutes.

Sticky Apples with Walnuts

(Prep + Cook Time: 20 minutes / Servings: 4)

Ingredients:

3 large Apples, peeled and sliced
¼ cup Honey
¼ cup Maple Syrup
1/3 cup chopped Walnuts
1 tbsp Applesauce
½ cup Water
¼ tsp Cinnamon Powder

Directions:

Combine the water, honey, maple syrup, and cinnamon in the Crock Pot Express.

Stir in the apple slices.

Close the lid and cook on BEANS/CHILI for 7 minutes.

Allow the pressure to release naturally.

Stir in the applesauce and cook for 2 more minutes.

Release the pressure naturally.

Serve topped with walnuts.

Crunchy Chili Corn

(Prep + Cook Time: 45 minutes / Servings: 6)

Ingredients:

2 cups dried Corn, soaked overnight
1 tbsp Chili Powder
1 tsp Salt
2 tbsp Olive Oil

Directions:

Place the corn with the minimum requirement of water for the Crock Pot Express.

Close the lid and cook on MEAT/STEW for 35 minutes.

Allow the pressure to release naturally.

Drain the corn and pat dry on paper towels.

Heat the oil in the Crock Pot Express along with the spices.

Add corn and sauté for a few minutes.

Potato and Bacon Snack

(Prep + Cook Time: 25 minutes / Servings: 4)

Ingredients:

1 pound Potatoes
4 Bacon Slices, chopped

1 tsp Garlic Salt
¼ tsp Pepper
4 tbsp Sour Cream
¼ cup Chicken Broth
1 ½ cup Water

Directions:

Combine the water and potatoes in the Crock Pot Express.

Close the lid and cook on BEANS/CHILI for 15 minutes.

Dice the potatoes and place in a bowl.

Add the bacon slices in the Crock Pot Express and cook until crisp on BEANS/CHILI. Add the bacon to the bowl and stir to combine. Whisk together the sour cream, broth, and spices. Drizzle over the potatoes.

Corn Pudding

(Prep + Cook Time: 40 minutes / Servings: 4)

Ingredients:

1 cup Corn Kernels
2 Shallots, chopped
2 Eggs, beaten
¼ cup Sour Cream
3 tbsp Cornmeal
¾ cup Milk
1 ½ cups Water
1 tbsp Sugar
Salt and Pepper, to taste

Directions:

Coat the Crock Pot Express with cooking spray.

Add shallots and cook for a few minutes until soft. Transfer to a bowl.

Stir in the remaining ingredients, except the water.

Transfer to a baking dish and cover with foil.

Pour the water in the Crock Pot Express and lower the trivet.

Add the baking dish and close the lid.

Cook on MEAT/STEW for 30 minutes.

Release the pressure naturally.

Hardboiled Eggs

(Prep + Cook Time: 10 minutes / Servings: 6)

Ingredients:

6 Eggs
1 ½ cups Water

Directions:

Pour the water in your Crock Pot Express and add the eggs.

Close the lid.

Set the Multi-Cooker to RICE/RISOTTO and cook for 6 minutes. Release the pressure naturally.

Place the eggs in an ice bath for 2 minutes. Peel and serve,

Yogurt Custard

(Prep + Cook Time: 30 minutes / Servings: 6)

Ingredients:

1 cup Yogurt
2 tsp Cardamom Powder
1 cup Water
1 cup Milk
1 cup Condensed Milk

Directions:

Pour the water in your Crock Pot Express.

In a pan, combine the rest of the ingredients.

Cover the pan with foil and place it in the Crock Pot Express.

Close the lid and cook on YOGURT for 20 minutes.

Do a natural pressure release for 10 minutes.

Cinnamon Squash Snack

(Prep + Cook Time: 20 minutes / Servings: 6)

Ingredients:

1 pound Acorn Squash, halved
1 tsp Baking Soda
1 cup Water
1 tsp Cinnamon
2 tbsp Apple Cider Vinegar
½ cup Butter, melted
½ tsp Salt

Directions:

Sprinkle the squash with salt with cinnamon and salt.

Pour the water in the Crock Pot Express and stir in the baking soda.

Add the squash. Drizzle with vinegar and butter.

Close the lid and cook on STEAM for 10 minutes.

Release the pressure naturally.

Spicy Sweet Potato Cubes

(Prep + Cook Time: 15 minutes / Servings: 6)

Ingredients:

6 Large Sweet Potatoes, cubed
2 tbsp Butter, melted
1 tsp Chili Powder
¼ tsp Pepper
½ tsp Salt
¼ tsp Cayenne Pepper
¼ tsp Turmeric Powder
1 tbsp grated Parmesan Cheese
1 ½ cups Water

Directions:

Pour the water in your Crock Pot Express.

Place the potatoes in the steamer basket.

Close the lid and cook on SOUP for 10 minutes.

Allow the pressure to release naturally.

Sprinkle the potatoes with the spices, drizzle with butter, and top with grated parmesan.

Divide between 6 small serving bowls and enjoy!

Mini Pumpkin Puddings

(Prep + Cook Time: 120 minutes / Servings: 4)

Ingredients:

1 cup Pumpkin Puree
1 tbsp Butter
1 Egg, beaten
1 Egg Yolk
¼ cup Half and Half
¼ cup Sugar
½ tsp Cinnamon
½ tsp Vanilla
¼ tsp Ginger
1 cup Water
Pinch of Salt

Directions:

Pour the water in the Crock Pot Express and lower the trivet.

Whisk all of the ingredients together.

Divide the mixture between 4 ramekins.

Place the ramekins in the cooker.

Close the lid and cook for 18 minutes on MEAT/STEW.

Release the pressure naturally.

Let pudding cool for 1 ½ hours before serving.

Salmon Bites

(Prep + Cook Time: 15 minutes / Servings: 4)

Ingredients:

1 can Salmon, flaked
1 Spring Onion, minced
1 cup Breadcrumbs
½ cup Cream Cheese
1 tbsp chopped Parsley
¼ tsp Salt
¼ tsp Pepper
1 tbsp Butter
½ cup Tomato Sauce
1 cup Water

Directions:

Combine the first 7 ingredients in a bowl. Make balls out of the mixture.

Melt the butter in the Crock Pot Express on MEAT/STEW.

Add the balls and cook until golden on all sides.

Transfer to a baking dish and pour the tomato sauce over.

Pour the water in your Crock Pot Express and lower the trivet. Place the dish inside and close the lid.

Cook for 4 minutes. Release the pressure naturally.

Three-Cheese Small Macaroni Cups

(Prep + Cook Time: 15 minutes / Servings: 8)

Ingredients:

½ pound Elbow Macaroni
2 cups Water
4 ounces shredded Cheddar Cheese
4 ounces shredded Monterey Jack Cheese
¼ cup shredded Parmesan Cheese
2 tbsp Butter
½ can Evaporated Milk

Directions:

Combine the water, butter, macaroni, salt, and pepper, in the Crock Pot Express.

Close the lid and cook for 7 minutes on RICE/RISOTTO.

Allow the pressure to release naturally and stir in the milk and cheeses. Close the lid again and cook for additional minute. Divide between 8 cups.

Chili Sriracha Eggs

(Prep + Cook Time: 20 minutes / Servings: 6)

Ingredients:

6 Eggs
½ tsp Chili Powder
1 ½ tbsp Sour Cream
1 tbsp Mayonnaise
Pinch of Pepper
1 tsp Sriracha
1 tbsp grated Parmesan Cheese

Directions:

Combine the eggs and water in the Crock Pot Express.

Close the lid and cook on RICE/RISOTTO for 6 minutes.

Let cool before peeling. Whisk together the sour cream, mayonnaise, pepper, chili powder, and sriracha.

Cut the eggs in half and top with the mixture.

Sprinkle the parmesan cheese over.

Vegetarian and Vegan

Potato and Pea Bowl

(Prep + Cook Time: 25 minutes / Servings: 4)

Ingredients:

3 Sweet Potatoes, chopped
1 Onion, chopped
1 cup Peas
2 cups chopped Spinach
2 tsp Garlic
1 tbsp Tomato Paste
1 tbsp Oil
½ tsp Coriander
1 tsp Cumin
1 ½ cups Water

Directions:

Heat the oil in the Crock Pot Express on BROWN/SAUTÉ.

Cook the onions and garlic for 2 minutes. Whisk in the tomato paste and spices. Stir in the water and tomato paste.

Add the sweet potatoes and cook for 14 minutes.

Allow the pressure to release naturally. Add the spinach and cook until wilted.

Saucy Barbecue Veggie Meal

(Prep + Cook Time: 20 minutes / Servings: 4)

Ingredients:

2 Tomatoes, chopped
2 Carrots, chopped
1 cup Peas
2 Onions, chopped
1 cup chopped Parsnips
2 Bell Peppers, diced

2 Sweet Potatoes, diced
1/3 cup BBQ Sauce
1 tbsp Oil
1 tbsp Ketchup
¼ tsp Cayenne Pepper
½ tsp Salt
¼ tsp Pepper
1 cup Veggie Stock

Directions:

Heat the oil in your Crock Pot Express.

Add onions and cook for 2 minutes on BROWN/SAUTÉ mode.

Add parsnips and carrots and cook for 3 more minutes.

Stir in the remaining ingredients. Close the lid and cook for 10 minutes. Allow the pressure to release naturally.

Discard the excess cooking liquid.

Garlicky and Chili Pomodoro Zoodles

(Prep + Cook Time: 15 minutes / Servings: 4)

Ingredients:

2 Large Zucchini, spiralized
½ Onion, diced
3 tsp minced Garlic
1 tbsp Olive Oil
1 cup diced Tomatoes
¾ cup Tomato Sauce
1 tbsp chopped Basil
2 tsp Chili Powder
Salt and Pepper, to taste

Directions:

Heat the oil in your Crock Pot Express on BROWN/SAUTÉ.

Cook the onions for 3 minutes. Add garlic and cook for 1 more minute. Stir in the tomatoes and tomato sauce.

Close the lid and cook for 3 minutes. Release the pressure naturally.

Stir in the zoodles and season with salt and pepper.

Close the lid and cook for 3 more minutes.

Stir in the chili powder.

Serve topped with chopped basil.

Cheesy Sour Veggie Casserole

(Prep + Cook Time: 35 minutes / Servings: 8)

Ingredients:

6 Potatoes, chopped
½ cup chopped Onion
1 cup chopped Carrots
1 cup chopped Bell Peppers
1 cup Panko Breadcrumbs
½ cup Sour Cream
1 cup shredded Cheddar Cheese
3 tbsp Butter, melted
2 tbsp Olive Oil

Directions:

Heat the oil in the Crock Pot Express on BROWN/SAUTÉ.

Cook the onions for 2 minutes.

Add the veggies and cook for 2 more minutes. Pour enough water to cover.

Close and cook for 7 minutes.

Transfer to a baking pan, but leave the liquid in the Crock Pot Express.

Lower the trivet.

In the baking pan, stir in the remaining ingredients.

Place the pan in the Crock Pot Express and cook for 5 more minutes.

Scallion Porridge

(Prep + Cook Time: 15 minutes / Servings: 4)

Ingredients:

1 ½ cups Oats
3 cups Water
½ cup chopped Scallions
½ tsp Salt
½ cup Savory Cashew Cream

Directions:

Combine the water, scallions, salt, and oats in your Crock Pot Express.

Close the lid and cook for 8 minutes on RICE/RISOTTO.

Release the pressure naturally. Top with the cashew cream.

Eggplant and Olive Toast

(Prep + Cook Time: 30 minutes / Servings: 6)

Ingredients:

6 toasted Bread Sliced
2 Eggplants, peeled and sliced
2 Garlic Cloves
A handful of Black Olives
2 tbsp Olive Oil
1 tbsp Tahini
Juice from 1 Lemon
Pinch of Red Pepper Flakes
½ tsp Salt
¼ tsp Pepper
1 ½ cups Water

Directions:

Combine the water and eggplant in the Crock Pot Express.

Close the lid and cook on BROWN/SAUTÉ for 6 minutes.

Drain and place the eggplants in a food processor.

Add the lemon juice, olive oil, olives, garlic, salt, pepper, and pepper flakes. Pulse until smooth. Spread the mixture over the toast.

Crock Pot Express Peperonata

(Prep + Cook Time: 15 minutes / Servings: 4)

Ingredients:

1 Green Bell Pepper, sliced
2 Yellow Bell Peppers, sliced
2 Red Bell Peppers, sliced
3 Tomatoes, chopped
1 Red Onions, chopped
2 Garlic Cloves, minced
1 cup Veggie Stock
2 tbsp Olive Oil
Salt and Pepper, to taste
4 cup cooked Egg Noodles

Directions:

Heat the oil in the Crock Pot Express on BROWN/SAUTÉ.

Cook the onion for 2 minutes. Add peppers and cook for 2 more minutes.

Add garlic and cook for 1 minute.

Stir in the tomatoes and cook for 2 minutes before adding the stock.

Close the lid and cook for 4 minutes. Drain and serve over noodles.

Curried Coconut Potatoes and Chickpeas with Almonds

(Prep + Cook Time: 30 minutes / Servings: 4)

Ingredients:

5 large Potatoes, diced
1 cup canned Chickpeas, drained
1 Red Onions, chopped
2 ounces toasted Almonds, chopped

2 tbsp Curry Paste
1 cup Coconut Milk
½ cup Water
1 tbsp Coconut Oil
Salt and Pepper, to taste

Directions:

Melt the coconut oil in the Crock Pot Express on BROWN/SAUTÉ. Add onion and cook for 3 minutes.

Whisk in the coconut milk, water, and curry paste.

Stir in the potatoes, chickpeas, and season with salt and pepper. Close the lid and cook for 5 minutes.

Serve topped with almonds.

Lentil and Currant Meal Salad

(Prep + Cook Time: 25 minutes / Servings: 6)

Ingredients:

3 cups dry Lentils
2 ½ cups canned Peas, drained
1 cup chopped Tomatoes
1 cup chopped Scallions
¼ cup Champagne Vinegar
¼ cup Tamari
1 tbsp Oil
1 tsp minced Garlic
Salt and Pepper, to taste

Directions:

Place the lentils in your Crock Pot Express and add enough water to cover them.

Close the lid and cook on BEANS/CHILI for 15 minutes.

Allow the pressure to release naturally. Transfer the lentils to a bowl. Whisk together the tamari, garlic, oil, and vinegar.

Place the vinegar and remaining ingredients in the bowl with lentils. Mix to coat well.

Gingery Stuffed Potatoes

(Prep + Cook Time: 35 minutes / Servings: 5)

Ingredients:

10 Baby Potatoes
10 Cashews, soaked in almond milk
2 Tomatoes, pureed
1 Onion, diced
2 tbsp Coconut Oil
2 tsp ground Ginger
1 tsp Cumin
1 tsp Chili Powder
1 tsp Coriander
½ tsp Salt

Directions:

Peel and core the potatoes and reserve the carved-out flesh.

Melt the coconut oil in your Crock Pot Express on BROWN/SAUTÉ.

Cook the onion for 2 minutes. Add ginger and cook for 1 more. Add the spices, carved out potato flesh, and tomato.

Cook for 2 minutes. Press STOP and fill the potatoes with the tomato gravy.

Arrange the potatoes in the Crock Pot Express and add 1 cup of water.

Close the lid and cook for 10 minutes on MEAT/STEW.

Vegan Sausage and Pepper Casserole

(Prep + Cook Time: 30 minutes / Servings: 4)

Ingredients:

2 Vegan Sausage Links, sliced
2 Large Potatoes, diced
3 Bell Peppers, chopped
1 Onion, chopped
1 Zucchini, grated
1 Carrot, grated
½ cup Almond Milk

1 cup Veggie Stock
½ tsp Cumin
¼ tsp Pepper
¼ tsp Salt
¼ tsp Turmeric Powder
1 tbsp Olive Oil

Directions:

Heat the oil in your Crock Pot Express and BROWN/SAUTÉ the onions for 1 minute. Add peppers and cook for 4 more minutes. Add sausage and cook until browned.

Stir in the spices, stock, and potatoes.

Cover and cook for 5 minutes on MEAT/STEW.

Stir in the remaining ingredients. Cook for 3 more minutes.

Drain and serve.

Stir in the rest of the ingredients.

Honey and Gingery Squash Spaghetti

(Prep + Cook Time: 40 minutes / Servings: 4-6)

Ingredients:

3-pound Spaghetti Squash
1 cup Honey
1 cup Water
½ cup Brown Sugar
2 tbsp grated Ginger
2 tbsp Coconut Oil
1 tbsp Veggie Stock Cube
¼ tsp Salt

Directions:

Pour the water in your Crock Pot Express and lower the basket. Add the squash in the basket.

Close the lid and cook on MEAT/STEW for 25 minutes.

Cut in half and let cool for a few minutes.

Meanwhile, discard the water and melt the coconut oil in your Crock Pot Express.

Add ginger and cook until fragrant. Whisk in the remaining ingredients. Scrape the squash noodles with a fork and serve topped with the glaze.

Flavorful Tofu Bowl

(Prep + Cook Time: 10 minutes / Servings: 6)

Ingredients:

20 ounces Firm Tofu, cubed
2 tsp minced Garlic
1 Onion, chopped
2 tbsp chopped Chives
1 tsp minced Ginger
2 cups Veggie Broth
2 tbsp Tamari
2 tbsp White or Mirin Wine
3 tsp Canola Oil
2 cups cooked Rice or Quinoa

Directions:

Heat the oil in your Crock Pot Express on BROWN/SAUTÉ.

Add tofu and cook until browned.

Place the remaining ingredients, except the rice, in a food processor and pulse until smooth.

Pour this mixture over the tofu. Close the lid and cook on STEAM for 2 minutes. Release the pressure naturally. Stir in the rice and serve.

Tempeh Sandwiches

(Prep + Cook Time: 30 minutes / Servings: 4)

Ingredients:

12 ounces Tempeh, sliced
6 Brioche Buns
1 tsp minced Ginger

2 tbsp Brown Mustard
2 tsp Agave Nectar
1 tsp minced Garlic
½ tsp Smoked Paprika
½ cup Apple Cider Vinegar
1/3 cup Veggie Stock
2 tbsp Tamari
Salt and Pepper, to taste

Directions:

Coat the Crock Pot Express with cooking spray and sauté the tempeh on BROWN/SAUTÉ for a few minutes.

Stir in the remaining ingredients, except the buns, and close the lid. Cook for 2 minutes.

Release the pressure naturally. Divide the mixture between the buns.

Tofu and Veggie 'Stir Fry'

(Prep + Cook Time: 20 minutes / Servings: 4)

Ingredients:

12 ounces Tofu, mashed
2 Shallots, diced
1 Tomato, diced
1 cup chopped Parsnips
2 tbsp Olive Oil
2 tsp Sherry
¼ cup chopped Parsley
1 tsp minced Garlic
3 cups Water
Salt and Pepper, to taste

Directions:

Heat the oil in the Crock Pot Express on BROWN/SAUTÉ.

Add shallots, parsnips, garlic, and tomatoes, and sauce for 3 minutes.

Add tofu, sherry, and season with salt and pepper.

Press STOP and close the lid. Choose STEAM and cook for 4 minutes.
Release the pressure naturally.

Mushroom and Veggie Baguette

(Prep + Cook Time: 20 minutes / Servings: 4)

Ingredients:

1 Baguette, cut into 4 equal pieces
1 ½ cups chopped Mushrooms
1 Shallot, chopped
1 Carrot, chopped
2 Bell Peppers, chopped
1 Parsnip, chopped
2 Tomatoes, chopped
1 Garlic Clove
1 tbsp Coconut Oil
1 1/3 cup Veggie Stock
Salt and Pepper, to taste

Directions:

Melt the coconut oil in your Crock Pot Express on RICE/RISOTTO. Add shallots and garlic and cook for 2 minutes.

Stir in the rest of the veggies and cook for 5 minutes.

Stir in the remaining ingredients and cook for 6 minutes, with the lid closed. Release the pressure naturally.

Transfer to a food processor and pulse until smooth.

Spread this mixture over the baguette.

Fruity Wheat Berry Lunch

(Prep + Cook Time: 30 minutes / Servings: 6)

Ingredients:

2 cups Wheat Berries
1/3 cup dried Cherries

1/3 cup dried Figs, chopped
2 Pears, peeled and diced
6 ½ cups Water
½ cup Almond Milk
½ tsp Pumpkin Spice

Directions:

Combine all the ingredients in your Crock Pot Express.

Cook on RICE/RISOTTO for 25 minutes.

Release the pressure naturally.

Drain the excess liquid and serve.

Sweet Potato and Marshmallow Casserole

(Prep + Cook Time: 30 minutes / Servings: 6)

Ingredients:

3 ½ pounds Sweet Potatoes, chopped
2 cups Water
1 tsp Cayenne Pepper
1 tsp Salt
¼ tsp Pepper

Topping:

1 ¾ cup Mini Marshmallows
2 ½ tbsp Coconut Oil, melted
1 cup Brown Sugar
1/3 cup chopped Walnuts
¼ tsp grated Nutmeg
½ cup Flour

Directions:

Place the potatoes, water, cayenne, salt, and pepper in the Multi-cooker.

Close the lid and cook on SOUP for 15 minutes.

Allow the pressure to release naturally.

Drain and transfer the potatoes to a baking dish.

Discard the water and whisk the topping ingredients, except the marshmallows, in the Crock Pot Express and cook for 1 minute on MEAT/STEW.

Drizzle the topping over the potatoes and top with marshmallows.

Pour 1 ½ cups water in the Crock Pot Express and lower the trivet.

Place the dish inside and cook on MEAT/STEW for about 5 minutes.

Apple and Red Cabbage Vegetarian Dinner

(Prep + Cook Time: 30 minutes / Servings: 4)

Ingredients:

1 pound Red Cabbage, shredded
½ cup Red Wine
1 cup diced Apples
1 cup diced Onions
1 tsp Thyme
1 ½ cups Veggie Stock
1 tbsp Coconut Oil
1 ½ tbsp Cornstarch Slurry
1 ½ tbsp Flour
Salt and Pepper, to taste
½ tsp Brown Sugar

Directions:

Melt the coconut oil in Crock Pot Express on BROWN/SAUTÉ.

Add onions and apples and cook for 5 minutes

Stir in the remaining ingredients, except the slurry.

Close the lid and cook for 15 minutes.

Press the MEAT/STEW button and bring the mixture to a boil.

Stir in the slurry and cook uncovered until thickened.

Vegan Fig Breakfast

(Prep + Cook Time: 20 minutes / Servings: 2)

Ingredients:

1 ½ cups Steel Cut Oats
½ cup dried Figs, chopped
1 tbsp Coconut Oil
2 tbsp Agave Nectar
¾ cup Fresh Orange Juice
4 cups Water
1/3 tsp Cinnamon

Directions:

Add one cup of water in the Crock Pot Express.

Combine the remaining ingredients in a pan.

Place the pan inside the Crock Pot Express.

Close the lid and cook on STEW for 10 minutes.

Release the pressure naturally.

Vegetable and Side Dishes

Swiss Chard with Pumpkin Seeds

(Prep + Cook Time: 30 minutes / Servings: 4)

Ingredients:

7 cups chopped Swiss Chard
1 cup Stock
¼ cup chopped Red Onions
2 Garlic Cloves, minced
1 tbsp Pumpkin Seeds
1 cup Water
3 tsp Canola Oil
Salt and Pepper, to taste

Directions:

Heat the oil in the Crock Pot Express on BEANS/CHILI.

Cook the onions and garlic for 2 minutes.

Stir in the stock and chard. Close the lid and cook for 7 minutes. Serve topped with pumpkin seeds.

Prosciutto Collards

(Prep + Cook Time: 20 minutes / Servings: 6)

Ingredients:

1 ½ cups chopped Collards
1 ½ cups diced Scallions
2 Garlic Cloves, minced
1 pound Prosciutto, diced
2 ½ cups Stock
Salt and Pepper, to taste

Directions:

Place the prosciutto and scallions in your Crock Pot Express and brown them on STEAM.

Stir in the remaining ingredients.

Close the lid and cook for 10 minutes.

Release the pressure naturally.

Garlicky Edamame

(Prep + Cook Time: 5 minutes / Servings: 4)

Ingredients:

2 cups Edamame
2 tsp minced Garlic
1 tbsp Soy Sauce
1 cup Water
1 tsp Olive Oil
Pinch of Salt
Pinch of Pepper

Directions:

Heat the oil in your Crock Pot Express and cook the garlic until fragrant.

Transfer to a steaming basket along with the edamame.

Pour the water in the Crock Pot Express and insert the steaming basket.

Close the lid and cook for 3 minutes

Stir in the remaining ingredients.

Rosemary and Garlic Potatoes

(Prep + Cook Time: 30 minutes / Servings: 4)

Ingredients:

2 pounds Baby Potatoes
4 tsp Oil
½ cup Stock
2 tsp minced Garlic
1 ½ tsp dried Rosemary
Salt and Pepper, to taste

Directions:

Heat the oil in your Crock Pot Express and add the potatoes, garlic, and rosemary.

Sprinkle with salt and pepper and cook for 8 minutes.

Stir in the stock and close the lid.

Cook for 8 minutes on RICE/RISOTTO.

Release the pressure naturally for 10 minutes.

Buttery Golden Beets

(Prep + Cook Time: 30 minutes / Servings: 4)

Ingredients:

4 Golden Beets, trimmed
2 tbsp Butter, melted
¾ cup Water
Salt and Pepper, to taste

Directions:

Pour the water in your Crock Pot Express.

Place the beets in the steaming basket and cook for 15 minutes on MEAT/ STEW.

Let the beets cool for a few minutes, before slicing them.

Drizzle with butter and season with salt and pepper.

Creamy Potato Salad

(Prep + Cook Time: 55 minutes / Servings: 6)

Ingredients:

1 ½ pound Potatoes, chopped
2 Carrots, chopped
2 small Leeks, chopped
1 cup chopped Celery
1/3 cup Mayonnaise
2 tsp Vinegar

2 cups Water
Salt and Pepper, to taste

Directions:

Place the potatoes, carrots, celery, leeks, and water in the Crock Pot Express and cook on STEW for 10 minutes.

Release the pressure naturally. Drain and transfer to a bowl. Whisk together the remaining ingredients. Pour over the potatoes and stir to combine.

Paprika Hash Browns

(Prep + Cook Time: 20 minutes / Servings: 4)

Ingredients:

1 pound Potatoes, grated
1 tsp Smoked Paprika
1 ½ tbsp Butter
1 ½ tbsp Corn Oil
½ tsp Pepper
1 tsp Salt

Directions:

Melt the butter along with the oil in the Crock Pot Express on BROWN/SAUTÉ.

Add potatoes and cook for 6 minutes. Stir in the remaining ingredients.

Press the potatoes with a metal spatula and close the lid.

Release the pressure immediately. Stir in the paprika and serve.

Basil Eggplant Side

(Prep + Cook Time: 40 minutes / Servings: 4)

Ingredients:

2 cups cubed Eggplants
1/3 cup Olive Oil
½ cup chopped Basil
2 tsp minced Garlic
1 cup sliced Red Onion

2 tbsp Red Wine Vinegar
1 tbsp Salt

Directions:

Sprinkle the eggplants with the salt and place them in a colander for 20 minutes. Rinse and squeeze them, reserving the liquid.

Heat the oil in the Crock Pot Express and press STEAM.

Cook the eggplants, garlic, and onion for a few minutes.

Stir in the wine and reserved liquid. Close the lid and cook for 7 minutes. Release the pressure naturally. Serve with basil.

Cauliflower and Egg Salad

(Prep + Cook Time: 5 minutes / Servings: 4)

Ingredients:

2 ½ cups Cauliflower Florets
2 Hardboiled Eggs, sliced
¾ cup Water

Dressing:

1 ½ tbsp Mayonnaise
1 ½ tbsp Parmesan Cheese
4 tbsp Olive Oil
1 Garlic Clove, minced
1 canned Anchovy, chopped
¼ tsp Mustard
¾ tbsp Lemon Juice
Salt and Pepper, to taste

Directions:

Place the cauliflower and water in your Crock Pot Express.

Cook for 2 minutes on RICE/RISOTTO.

Drain and transfer to a bowl. Whisk together the dressing ingredients and pour over the cauliflower.

Toss to coat. Serve topped with egg slices.

Orange Broccoli Parmesan

(Prep + Cook Time: 5 minutes / Servings: 4)

Ingredients:

2 cups Broccoli Florets
¼ cup grated Parmesan Cheese
1 tbsp Orange Juice
¾ cup Water
2 tbsp Butter, melted
Pinch of Salt

Directions:

Place the water and broccoli in the Crock Pot Express.

Cook on RICE/RISOTTO or 2 minutes.

Release the pressure naturally and transfer the florets to a bowl.

Add the remaining ingredients and toss to combine.

Simple Mediterranean Asparagus

(Prep + Cook Time: 5 minutes / Servings: 4)

Ingredients:

1 pound Asparagus Spears
1 Garlic Clove, minced
1 tbsp minced Shallot
2 ½ tbsp Olive Oil
1 tbsp Lemon Juice
½ cup Water

Directions:

Place the asparagus and water in your Crock Pot Express.

Cook for 3 minutes on STEAM. Release the pressure naturally.

Toss the asparagus with the remaining ingredients to combine.

Spicy Cauliflower with Peas

(Prep + Cook Time: 25 minutes / Servings: 8)

Ingredients:

2 Tomatoes, diced
2 ¼ cups Peas
2 pounds Cauliflower, broken into florets
2 tbsp minced Garlic
7 cups Stock
2 Yams, cubed
2 tbsp Butter
½ tsp Salt
¼ tsp Pepper
½ tsp Paprika
½ tsp Chili Powder
¼ tsp Red Pepper Flakes
¼ tsp Cayenne Pepper
½ tsp Onion Powder

Directions:

Melt the butter in the Crock Pot Express on RICE/RISOTTO and cook the garlic and spices for 1 minute. Stir in the remaining ingredients.

Close the lid and cook for 10 minutes.

Drain and serve the veggies.

Rutabaga and Scallion Side

(Prep + Cook Time: 10 minutes / Servings: 4)

Ingredients:

1 cup minced Scallions
2 Rutabagas, cubed
1 cup Water
3 tsp Orange Juice
½ tsp Cayenne Pepper
¼ cup Olive Oil
¼ tsp Salt

Directions:

Combine the water and rutabaga in the Crock Pot Express and close the lid.

Cook on BEANS/CHILI for 5 minutes.

Transfer to a bowl.

Release the pressure naturally.

Combine the remaining ingredients and pour over the rutabaga.

Toss to combine.

Herbal Mashed Sweet Potatoes

(Prep + Cook Time: 20 minutes / Servings: 6)

Ingredients:

2 pounds Sweet Potatoes, chopped
½ Butter Stick, chopped
¾ cup Milk
1 tsp Thyme
1 tsp Marjoram
2 tsp Rosemary
¼ tsp Parsley
Salt and Pepper, to taste

Directions:

Place the potatoes in the Crock Pot Express and cover with water.

Cook on MEAT/STEW for 10 minutes. Release the pressure naturally. Mash the potatoes with a masher in a bowl.

Stir in the remaining ingredients.

Yam and Corn Side

(Prep + Cook Time: 20 minutes / Servings: 6)

Ingredients:

1 pound Yams, peeled and cubed
¾ pound frozen Corn

1 tsp minced Garlic
3 tsp Olive Oil
¼ tsp minced Ginger
½ tsp Seasoning by choice
Salt and Pepper, to taste

Directions:

Place the yams in the Crock Pot Express and add enough water to cover them.

Close and cook for 10 minutes on STEAM.

Allow the pressure to release naturally and stir in the corn.

Close and cook for 3 more minutes.

Transfer to a bowl and stir in the remaining ingredients.

Citrusy Almond Potatoes

(Prep + Cook Time: 15 minutes / Servings: 4)

Ingredients:

10 large Potatoes, cubed
¾ cup chopped Almonds
2 Tangerines, sectioned
1 cup Mayonnaise
Juice of 1 Lime
1 tsp Orange Zest
½ tsp Allspice
1 tsp Salt
¼ tsp White Pepper
Pinch of Nutmeg
1 cup Water

Directions:

Combine the water, lime juice, and potatoes in the Crock Pot Express.

Close and cook on MEAT/STEW for 10 minutes.

Release the pressure naturally.

Transfer to a serving bowl.

Whisk together the spices, zest, and mayonnaise in a bowl.

Pour the mixture over the potatoes.

Add tangerines and almonds.

Flavorful Bell Peppers

(Prep + Cook Time: 15 minutes / Servings: 4)

Ingredients:

1 ½ pounds Bell Peppers
½ cup Stock
¾ cup Tomato Soup
½ cup chopped Scallions
½ tbsp Miso Paste
½ Butter Stick
1 tsp minced Garlic
2 tbsp Champagne Vinegar
Salt and Pepper, to taste

Directions:

Melt the butter in the Crock Pot Express on STEAM and cook the scallions for 3 minutes.

Add garlic and cook for a minute. Stir in the remaining ingredients. Close the lid and cook for 2 minutes. Release the pressure naturally.

Lime and Mayo Steamed Broccoli

(Prep + Cook Time: 15 minutes / Servings: 6)

Ingredients:

1 ½ pounds Broccoli, broken into florets
¼ cup Mayonnaise
¼ cup Lime Juice
¼ cup Mayonnaise
1 tsp Cayenne Pepper
¼ tsp Garlic Salt
1 cup Water

Directions:

Combine the water, lime juice, and broccoli in your Crock Pot Express.

Cook for 4 minutes on BEANS/CHILI on HIGH pressure.

Release the pressure naturally. Stir in the remaining ingredients.

Zesty Onions

(Prep + Cook Time: 15 minutes / Servings: 6)

Ingredients:

1 ½ pounds Onions
3 tbsp Sugar
¼ cup Wine Vinegar
2 tbsp Flour
1 cup Water
2 Bay Leaves
1 tsp Salt
½ tsp Pepper

Directions:

Combine the onions, bay leaves, and water in the Crock Pot Express.

Close the lid and cook on STEAM for 4 minutes.

Release the pressure naturally. Transfer to a platter.

Get rid of the cooking spray. Whisk together the remaining ingredients in the Crock Pot Express.

Cook for 2 minutes uncovered.Pour the sauce over the onions.

Mashed Root Veggies

(Prep + Cook Time: 30 minutes / Servings: 4)

Ingredients:

1 pound Potatoes, chopped
¼ pound Carrots, chopped
¾ pound Turnips, chopped

½ cup Heavy Cream
1 tsp Horseradish
2 tbsp Butter
Salt and Pepper, to taste

Directions:

Combine the veggies in the Crock Pot Express and add enough water to cover them. Close the lid and cook for 10 minutes on MEAT/STEW.

Drain and mash with a potato masher. Stir in the remaining ingredients.

Lemony Brussel Sprouts

(Prep + Cook Time: 30 minutes / Servings: 6)

Ingredients:

1 ½ pounds Brussel Sprouts
1 ¼ cup Water
½ Lemon, sliced
1 tbsp Butter, melted
Salt and Pepper, to taste

Directions:

Combine the lemon slices and Brussel sprouts in the Crock Pot Express. Add enough water to cover them.

Close the lid and cook for 2 minutes on RICE/RISOTTO.

Drizzle with butter and season with salt and pepper.

Balsamic Caper Beets

(Prep + Cook Time: 45 minutes / Servings: 4-6)

Ingredients:

4 Beets
1 tbsp Olive Oil
2 tbsp Capers
1 tsp minced Garlic
1 tbsp chopped Parsley

2 tbsp Balsamic Vinegar
Salt and Pepper, to taste

Directions:

Place the beets in the Crock Pot Express and cover with water.

Cook on MEAT/STEW for 20 minutes.

Release the pressure naturally and let the beets cool.

Whisk together the remaining ingredients.

Slice the beets and combine with the dressing.

Spinach with Cottage Cheese

(Prep + Cook Time: 25 minutes / Servings: 4)

Ingredients:

18 ounces chopped Spinach
10 ounces Cottage Cheese
1 Onion, chopped
8 Garlic Cloves, minced
1 tbsp Butter
2 tbsp Corn Flour
1 tsp Cumin
½ cup Water
½ tsp Coriander
1 tsp grated Ginger

Directions:

Melt the butter in the Crock Pot Express on BROWN/SAUTÉ. Cook the onions, ginger, and garlic for 2 minutes.

Stir in the spices and spinach and cook for 2 minutes.

Stir in the water and flour and close the lid.

Cook for 3 minutes. Stir in the cottage cheese.

Tamari Bok Choy

(Prep + Cook Time: 25 minutes / Servings: 3)

Ingredients:

1 Bok Choy Bunch, trimmed
2 tbsp Tamari
1 tsp minced Garlic
2 tbsp Olive Oil
1 cup Water
Salt and Pepper, to taste

Directions:

Heat the oil in the Crock Pot Express and cook the garlic for 1 minute on BROWN/SAUTÉ.

Add the remaining ingredients and close the lid.

Cook for 7 minutes.

Allow the pressure to release naturally.

Creamy Goat Cheese Cauliflower

(Prep + Cook Time: 30 minutes / Servings: 5)

Ingredients:

1 Cauliflower Head, cut into florets
2 tbsp Lemon Juice
2 tbsp Olive Oil
1 cup Vegetable Broth
2 tsp Red Pepper Flakes

Sauce:

6 ounces Goat Cheese
1 tsp Nutmeg
1/3 cup Heavy Cream
1 tbsp Olive Oil
Salt and Pepper, to taste

Directions:

Combine the lemon juice and cauliflower in your Crock Pot Express and cover with water.

Close and cook for 4 minutes on STEAM.

Release the pressure naturally and transfer to a plate.

Discard the cooking liquid and heat the oil in the Crock Pot Express.

Add red pepper flakes and cook until fragrant.

Add cauliflower and cook for 1 minute uncovered.

Return to the bowl.

Pulse all of the sauce ingredients in a food processor and pour over the cauliflower.

Sweet and Mustardy Carrots

(Prep + Cook Time: 20 minutes / Servings: 4)

Ingredients:

1 pound Carrots
2 tbsp Mustard
2 tbsp Butter
2 tbsp Honey
2 tsp minced Garlic
1 tsp Paprika
Salt and Pepper, to taste

Directions:

Place the carrots along with a cup of water in the Crock Pot Express.

Cook on RICE/RISOTTO for 10 minutes.

Release the pressure naturally.

Whisk together the remaining ingredients.

Brush over the carrots.

Kale and Carrot Side

(Prep + Cook Time: 15 minutes / Servings: 6)

Ingredients:

10 ounces chopped Kale
3 Carrots, sliced
½ Onion, chopped
½ cup Broth
1 tbsp Olive Oil
4 Garlic Cloves, minced
1 tbsp Lemon Juice
Salt and Pepper, to taste

Directions:

Heat the oil in the Crock Pot Express on RICE/RISOTTO.

Add garlic and cook for a minute. Stir in the remaining ingredients. Close the lid and cook for 10 minutes.

Release the pressure naturally. Drain and serve.

Zucchini and Cherry Tomato Delight

(Prep + Cook Time: 20 minutes / Servings: 8)

Ingredients:

1 pound Cherry Tomatoes
2 small Onion, chopped
6 medium Zucchinis, chopped
1 ½ tsp minced Garlic
1 tbsp Olive Oil
1 cup Water
2 tbsp chopped Basil
Salt and Pepper, to taste

Directions:

Heat the oil in the Crock Pot Express on BROWN/SAUTÉ.

Add onions and cook for 3 minutes. Add garlic and cook for 1 minute.

Stir in the tomatoes and zucchini and cook for 2 minutes.

Pour the water over. Close the lid and cook for 5 minutes.

Allow the pressure to release naturally.

Stir in the basil and season with salt and pepper.

Mushroom and Zucchini Platter

(Prep + Cook Time: 25 minutes / Servings: 8)

Ingredients:

12 ounces Mushrooms, sliced
4 medium Zucchinis, sliced
15 ounces canned Tomatoes with Juice
1 cup chopped Onion
1 Garlic Clove, minced
1 tbsp chopped Parsley
¼ tsp Red Pepper Flakes
2 tbsp Butter

Directions:

Melt the butter in your Crock Pot Express on BROWN/SAUTÉ. Add onion and garlic and cook for 2 minutes.

Add mushrooms and cook for 5 minutes.

Add tomatoes and zucchini and close the lid. Cook for 2 minutes.

Release the pressure naturally.

Stir in parsley and red pepper flakes and season.

Cabbage and Pepper Side

(Prep + Cook Time: 20 minutes / Servings: 8)

Ingredients:

2 pounds Cabbage, shredded
1 cup diced sliced Bell Peppers
¼ cup White Wine

½ cup Veggie Stock
1 cup chopped Scallions
¼ cup chopped Parsley
1 tbsp Oil
½ tsp Salt
¼ tsp Pepper

Directions:

Heat the oil in your Crock Pot Express on STEAM.

Add scallions and cook until soft.

Stir in the remaining ingredients.

Close the lid and cook for 10 minutes.

Release the pressure naturally.

Serve topped with parsley.

Cabbage with Bacon and Granny Smith Apples

(Prep + Cook Time: 15 minutes / Servings: 8)

Ingredients:

4 slices Smoked Bacon, chopped
4 tbsp Raisins
2 Granny Smith Apples, diced
1 pound Cabbage, shredded
¼ cup Sweet Red Wine
3 tbsp Brown Sugar
½ cup Water

Directions:

Cook the bacon in the Crock Pot Express until crispy on BROWN/SAUTÉ.

Add cabbage and apples and cook for 5 minutes.

Stir in the remaining ingredients.

Close the lid and cook on MEAT/STEW for 3 minutes.

Cheesy Broccoli Mash

(Prep + Cook Time: 20 minutes / Servings: 4)

Ingredients:

1 pound Potatoes, chopped
1 pound Broccoli, broken into florets
½ cup Milk
½ cup shredded Cheddar Cheese
Salt and Pepper, to taste

Directions:

Place the potatoes in the Crock Pot Express and cover with water.

Close the lid and cook on MEAT/STEW for 8 minutes.

Release the pressure naturally.

Add the broccoli and cook for 3-4 more minutes.

Release the pressure naturally again.

Drain and mash with a potato masher.

Stir in the remaining ingredients and serve.

Frascati and Sage Broccoli

(Prep + Cook Time: 15 minutes / Servings: 6)

Ingredients:

1 ½ pounds Broccoli, broken into florets
1 large Sweet Onion, sliced
1/3 cup Frascati
2 tsp Sage
3 tsp Olive Oil
1 tsp Garlic Paste
Salt and Pepper, to taste

Directions:

Heat the oil on BROWN/SAUTÉ and cook the onions until soft.

Add garlic paste and cook until fragrant.

Stir in the remaining ingredients. Add some water, if needed.

Close the lid and cook for 4 minutes.

Allow the pressure to release naturally and serve.

Sweet Caramelized Onions

(Prep + Cook Time: 15 minutes / Servings: 4)

Ingredients:

2 large Sweet Onions, peeled
1 tbsp Brown Sugar
2 tbsp Butter
1 ½ cup Water

Directions:

Place the water and onions in your Crock Pot Express and cook on BROWN/ SAUTÉ for 5 minutes.

Place in an ice bath for 2 minutes.

Slice and get rid of the cooking liquid.

Melt the butter in the Crock Pot Express and add the onions and sugar.

Cook for 5 minutes.

Mustardy Potato and Green Bean Salad

(Prep + Cook Time: 20 minutes / Servings: 8)

Ingredients:

2 pounds Potatoes, sliced
2 pounds Green Beans, trimmed
¼ cup Olive Oil
3 tsp Thyme
3 tbsp Lemon Juice
2 tbsp Mustard
Salt and Pepper, to taste

Directions:

Add the potatoes in the Crock Pot Express and cover with water.

Close the lid and cook on MEAT/STEW for 5 minutes.

Allow the pressure to release naturally and add the beans.

Cook for another 5 minutes.

Whisk together the remaining ingredients.

Pour the dressing over the salad and toss to combine.

Cauliflower Side with Pomegranate and Walnuts

(Prep + Cook Time: 20 minutes / Servings: 8)

Ingredients:

2 cups Pomegranate Seeds
3 medium Cauliflower Heads, broken into florets
¼ cup Hazelnuts, toasted
1 tbsp Capers
3 tbsp Olive Oil
3 tbsp Orange Juice

Directions:

Add 1 cup of water in the Crock Pot Express and place the cauliflower in the steaming basket.

Cook for 2 minutes on RICE/RISOTTO.

Release the pressure naturally and transfer to a bowl.

Stir in the remaining ingredients and serve.

Turmeric Kale with Shallots

(Prep + Cook Time: 20 minutes / Servings: 3)

Ingredients:

10 ounces Kale, chopped
5 Shallots, chopped
1 tsp Turmeric Powder

2 tsp Olive Oil
½ tsp Coriander Seeds
½ tsp Cumin
Salt and Pepper, to taste

Directions:

Pour 1 cup of water in the Crock Pot Express and place the kale in the steaming basket.

Close the lid and cook on STEAM for 2 minutes.

Transfer to a plate.

Discard the water and heat the oil in the Cooking Pot.

Add the spices and shallots and cook until soft.

Stir in the kale.

Spinach and Tomato Side

(Prep + Cook Time: 25 minutes / Servings: 6)

Ingredients:

10 cups Spinach
1 cup chopped Tomatoes
1 tbsp mince Garlic
1 Onion, diced
1 ¼ cup Veggie Broth
1 tbsp Lemon Juice
½ cup Tomato Puree
Salt and Pepper, to taste

Directions:

Coat the Crock Pot Express with cooking spray and cook the onion for a few minutes.

Add garlic and cook for one more minute.

Stir in the remaining ingredients and close the lid.

Cook for 3 minutes on MEAT/STEW.

Release the pressure naturally and serve.

Cajun Potatoes with Brussel Sprouts

(Prep + Cook Time: 20 minutes / Servings: 6)

Ingredients:

1 ½ pounds Potatoes, chopped
½ pound Brussel Sprouts, halved
1 tsp Cajun Seasoning
½ Onion, chopped
1 Garlic Clove, minced
1 ½ cup Chicken Stock
1 tbsp Oil

Directions:

Heat the oil in the Crock Pot Express on BROWN/SAUTÉ.

Cook the onions and garlic for 2 minutes,

Add the stock and potatoes and close the lid. Cook for 6 minutes.

Release the pressure, add the Brussel sprouts, and continue cooking for 4 more minutes.

Drain and transfer to a plate.

Season with Cajun seasoning.

Sour Cream Veggies with Bacon

(Prep + Cook Time: 20 minutes / Servings: 4)

Ingredients:

4 Bacon slices, chopped
2 Carrots, chopped
½ Onion, chopped
1 Garlic Clove, minced
2 Potatoes, chopped
1 cup Broccoli Florets
1 cup Cauliflower Florets
1 tbsp Lemon Juice
1 tbsp Olive Oil
1 cup Sour Cream

1 ½ cup Chicken Stock
Salt and Pepper, to taste

Directions:

Cook the bacon until crispy in the Crock Pot Express on BEANS/CHILI.

Add the onion and garlic and cook for 2 minutes.

Add the potatoes and carrots and cook for 2 more minutes.

Pour the stock over and close the lid.

Cook for 5 minutes.

Add the broccoli and cauliflower and cook for 4 more minutes.

Drain and transfer to a bowl.

Whisk together the remaining ingredients and pour over.

Beans and Grains

Cannellini Zucchini Salad

(Prep + Cook Time: 40 minutes / Servings: 6)

Ingredients:

2 ½ cups Cannellini Beans, soaked overnight
2 Zucchinis, peeled and diced
2 Garlic Cloves, minced
2 Shallots, chopped
1 can crushed Tomatoes
2 tbsp Oil
2 tsp Vinegar
4 ½ cups Water
Salt and Pepper, to taste
1 tbsp chopped Parsley

Directions:

Heat the oil in the Crock Pot Express on BEANS/CHILI.

Cook the onion and garlic for 2 minutes. Add beans and water and close the lid. Cook for 30 minutes.

Add zucchini and cook for 5 more. Drain and transfer to a bowl. Stir in the remaining ingredients.

Kidney Beans with Bacon and Tomatoes

(Prep + Cook Time: 35 minutes / Servings: 4)

Ingredients:

2 cups Kidney Beans, soaked overnight
1 ½ cups chopped Tomatoes
4 Bacon slices, diced
4 cups Water
½ cup Cumin
1 tsp Rosemary
Salt and Pepper, to taste

Directions:

Place the bacon in the Crock Pot Express and cook on BEANS/CHILI until crispy. Set aside.

Add tomatoes, cumin, and rosemary and cook for 2 minutes. Stir in the remaining ingredients and cook for 25 minutes.

Allow the pressure to release naturally. Transfer to a bowl and stir in the bacon.

Simple Lima Beans Under Pressure

(Prep + Cook Time: 20 minutes / Servings: 6)

Ingredients:

2 cups Lima Beans, soaked and rinsed
2 Garlic Cloves, minced
4 cups Water
3 tsp Oil
½ tsp Salt
¼ tsp Pepper

Directions:

Combine all the ingredients in your Crock Pot Express.

Close the lid and cook on BEANS/CHILI for 15 minutes. Allow the pressure to release naturally.

Navy Beans with Meat

(Prep + Cook Time: 25 minutes / Servings: 8)

Ingredients:

2 pounds canned Navy Beans
1 pound mixed Ground Meat
½ cup shredded Cheese
1 tsp minced Garlic
2 tbsp chopped Onion
1 tbsp Olive Oil
3 cups Water
Salt and Pepper, to taste

Directions:

Heat the oil in your Crock Pot Express on BROWN/SAUTÉ.

Add onion and garlic and cook for 2 minutes.

Add meat and cook until browned.

Stir the remaining ingredients and close the lid. Cook for 10 minutes. Release the pressure naturally and serve.

Bean Puree with Cilantro

(Prep + Cook Time: 25 minutes / Servings: 6)

Ingredients:

2 ¼ cups dry Pinto Beans, soaked
1 cup chopped Red Onions
2 ½ cups Water
1 ½ tsp Garlic Powder
1 tsp Chipotle Powder
½ cup Fresh Cilantro, chopped
3 tsp Oil
Salt and Pepper, to taste

Directions:

Heat the oil in the Crock Pot Express on BEANS/CHILI and cook the onions, garlic powder, chipotle, and cilantro for 3 minutes.

Stir in the beans and water and season with salt and pepper.

Cook for 20 minutes. Release the pressure naturally.

Mash the mixture with a potato masher.

Mushroom and Farro Beans

(Prep + Cook Time: 25 minutes / Servings: 4)

Ingredients:

1 ¼ cups Navy Beans
¾ cup Farro

2 ½ cups sliced Mushrooms
4 Green Onions, chopped
1 tsp minced Garlic
½ Jalapeno, minced
1 cup diced Tomatoes
2 ½ cups Broth

Directions:

Combine all of the ingredients in your Crock Pot Express.

Close the lid and cook on BEANS/CHILI for about 20 minutes.

Allow the pressure to release naturally.

Bean and Corn Salad

(Prep + Cook Time: 25 minutes / Servings: 4)

Ingredients:

2 cups Cannellini Beans, soaked overnight
1 cup chopped Red Onions
4 ½ cups Water
2 cans Corn
½ cup chopped Cilantro
2 tbsp minced Red Onion
1 tsp Cumin
1 tsp Chili Powder
1 tsp minced Garlic
¼ tbsp Olive Oil
Salt and Pepper, to taste

Directions:

Add the water and beans in your Crock Pot Express on BEANS/CHILI and cook for 20 minutes.

Allow the pressure to release naturally.

Drain the beans and transfer to a bowl. Stir in the remaining ingredients

Garbanzo Mash

(Prep + Cook Time: 20 minutes / Servings: 6)

Ingredients:

1 ¾ cup Garbanzo Beans
½ cup chopped Cilantro
¼ cup toasted Pumpkin Seeds
½ tbsp ground Mustard
2 tsp minced Garlic
1 Bay Leaf
Salt and Pepper, to taste

Directions:

Place the bay leaf and beans in your Crock Pot Express and cover with water.

Close the lid and cook on BEANS/CHILI for 10 minutes.

Allow the pressure to release naturally. Discard the bay leaf and drain the beans.

Transfer to a blender and add all of the other ingredients.

Blend until smooth.

Bean and Bacon Dip

(Prep + Cook Time: 20 minutes / Servings: 12)

Ingredients:

20 ounces frozen Lima beans
4 Bacon slices, cooked and crumbled
3 tsp Butter melted
½ tsp Cayenne Pepper
Salt and Pepper, to taste

Directions:

Place the beans in the Crock Pot Express and cover with water.

Close the lid and cook on BEANS/CHILI for 15 minutes.

Transfer to a food processor along with the remaining ingredients. Process until smooth.

Red Bean Salad

(Prep + Cook Time: 25 minutes / Servings: 4)

Ingredients:

1 cup dry Red Beans, soaked overnight and drained
½ cup chopped Onions
½ cup chopped Olives
1 cup sliced Tomatoes
2 Bay Leaves
½ tsp Maple Syrup
½ tsp Paprika
½ tsp Salt
¼ tsp Pepper
¼ cup chopped Mint
2 Garlic Cloves, mint
3 tsp Oil
1 tsp Chili Powder

Directions:

Place the beans in the Crock Pot Express and add enough water to cover them. Close the lid and cook on BEANS/CHILI for 20 minutes. Allow the pressure to release naturally.

Drain and transfer to a bowl along with the other ingredients.

Stir to combine.

Curried Chickpeas

(Prep + Cook Time: 40 minutes / Servings: 8)

Ingredients:

3 cups Chickpeas, soaked and rinsed
2 Tomatoes, chopped
2 Onions, chopped
2 tbsp Curry Powder
2 tbsp Oil
2 tsp minced Garlic
½ tsp Cumin

2 tsp Chipotle Powder
Salt and Pepper, to taste

Directions:

Place the chickpeas, salt, pepper, and 1 tbsp oil in the Cooking Pot. Cover with water and close the lid.

Cook for 30 minutes on BEANS/CHILI.

Allow the pressure to release naturally.

Stir in the remaining ingredients.

Cook for 5 more minutes.

Adzuki and Black Bean Salad

(Prep + Cook Time: 20 minutes / Servings: 6)

Ingredients:

1 ½ cups Black Beans, soaked overnight
1 ½ cups Adzuki Beans, soaked overnight
1 Onion, chopped
2 Bell Peppers, chopped
1 can Tomatoes
2 tbsp Oil
2 tsp Mustard
2 tsp Vinegar
1 tbsp Garlic Paste
1 tsp Thyme
Salt and Pepper, to taste

Directions:

Add the oil, onion, and beans to the Cooking Pot.

Add water to cover. Cook for 15 minutes on BEANS/CHILI.

Allow the pressure to release naturally.

Drain and transfer to a bowl. Stir in the remaining ingredients.

Place in the fridge until ready to serve.

Spicy Pinto and Navy Beans

(Prep + Cook Time: 35 minutes / Servings: 8)

Ingredients:

15 ounces Pinto Beans
15 ounces Navy Beans
1 tsp Chili Powder
1 tsp Onion Powder
1 tsp Garlic Powder
1/3 cup Olive Oil
1/3 cup chopped Scallions
1 tbsp Sesame Paste
1/3 cup Red Wine Vinegar
8 cups Water

Directions:

Combine all of the ingredients in the Crock Pot Express.

Close the lid and cook on BEANS/CHILI for 30 minutes.

Allow the pressure to release naturally.

Drain and transfer to a serving bowl.

Black Bean and Mushroom Spread

(Prep + Cook Time: 25 minutes / Servings: 6)

Ingredients:

2 cups Black Beans soaked and rinsed
1 cup sliced Porcini Mushrooms
1 cup chopped Red Onions
2 ½ cups Water
2 cups Beef Broth
1 ½ tsp Paprika
1 tbsp Butter
1 tsp Rosemary
½ tsp Cumin
Salt and Pepper

Directions:

Melt the butter in the Crock Pot Express and sauté the onions for a few minutes.

Add mushrooms and cook for 3 more minutes.

Stir in the remaining ingredients and close the lid.

Cook on BEANS/CHILI for 20 minutes. Allow the pressure to release naturally. Drain and transfer to a food processor.

Pulse until smooth.

Crunchy and Cheesy Beans

(Prep + Cook Time: 20 minutes / Servings: 6)

Ingredients:

16 ounces canned Beans
2 cups crushed Tortilla Chips
1 cup shredded Cheddar Cheese
1 cup diced Tomatoes
1 cup Tomato Sauce
¼ cup Water mixed with 1 tsp Cornstarch
1 tsp Chili Powder

Directions:

Place everything except the cheese in the Crock Pot Express.

Close the lid and cook for 5 minutes on BEANS/CHILI.

Allow the pressure to release naturally.

Stir in the cheese and cook uncovered for 5 more minutes.

Apricot and Raisin Oatmeal

(Prep + Cook Time: 15 minutes / Servings: 4)

Ingredients:

2 ¼ cups Water
1 ½ cups Steel Cut Oats
1 ½ cups Almond Milk

A handful of Raisins
8 Apricots, chopped
1 tsp Vanilla Paste
¾ cup Brown Sugar

Directions:

Combine all of the ingredients in your Crock Pot Express. Set it to RICE/RISOTTO, cover, and cook for 8 minutes.

Allow the pressure to release naturally.

Cinnamon Bulgur with Pecans

(Prep + Cook Time: 15 minutes / Servings: 8)

Ingredients:

2 cups Bulgur Wheat
¼ cup chopped Pecans
½ tsp Cloves
1 tsp Cinnamon
¼ tsp Nutmeg
1/3 cup Honey
6 cups Water

Directions:

Place all of the ingredients in your Crock Pot Express. Stir to combine well.

Close the lid and cook on BEANS/CHILI for 10 minutes.

Allow the pressure to release naturally.

Ham and Parmesan Grits

(Prep + Cook Time: 30 minutes / Servings: 6)

Ingredients:

1 cup Quick-Cooking Grits
1 cup grated Parmesan Cheese
10 ounces cooked Ham, diced
2 Eggs, whisked

½ Butter Stick
1 Shallot, chopped
1 tsp Paprika
Salt and Pepper, to taste
3 cups Water

Directions:

Melt the butter in the Crock Pot Express and brown the ham on RICE/RISOTTO.

Stir in the shallots and spices and cook for 2 minutes.

Add the grits and water and close the lid. Cook for 6 minutes.

Allow the pressure to release naturally and stir in the parmesan and eggs.

Close and cook for 3 more minutes.

Honey Polenta

(Prep + Cook Time: 15 minutes / Servings: 6)

Ingredients:

2 cups Polenta
½ Butter Stick
½ cup Honey
2 quarts Water
1 tsp Salt

Directions:

Combine all of the ingredients in your Crock Pot Express.

Close the lid and cook on RICE/RISOTTO for 8 minutes. Let the pressure drop naturally.

Rosemary Goat Cheese Barley

(Prep + Cook Time: 30 minutes / Servings: 6)

Ingredients:

2 cups Barley
6 cups Stock
1 Butter Stick, melted

1 cup chopped Spring Onions
½ cup Goat Cheese
¼ tsp Black Pepper
½ tsp Salt
2 tsp Rosemary

Directions:

Melt the butter in the Crock Pot Express on RICE/RISOTTO.

Add onions and cook until soft. Stir in the remaining ingredients, except the cheese.

Close the lid and cook for 25 minutes. Allow the pressure to release naturally. Stir in the goat cheese and serve.

Quinoa Salad

(Prep + Cook Time: 15 minutes / Servings: 8)

Ingredients:

2 cups Quinoa, rinsed and drained
2 Avocados, sliced
1 cup chopped Grapefruit
½ cup slivered Almonds
½ tsp Salt
3 tsp Oil
4 cups Water

Dressing:

½ cup Sour Cream
2 tbsp Lemon Juice
2 tbsp chopped Mint
2 tbsp Olive Oil

Directions:

Combine the quinoa and water in your Crock Pot Express and cook on RICE/RISOTTO for 8 minutes.

Transfer to a bowl and stir in the remaining ingredients.

Whisk together the dressing ingredients and pour over. Stir to coat well.

Banana and Fig Millet

(Prep + Cook Time: 20 minutes / Servings: 6)

Ingredients:

2 cups Millet
1 cup Milk
2 Bananas, sliced
¼ cup chopped dried Figs
½ tsp Vanilla
½ tsp Cinnamon
2 tbsp Coconut Oil
2 cups Water
Pinch of Salt

Directions:

Combine everything, except the bananas, in your Crock Pot Express.

Cook for 10 minutes on MEAT/STEW.

Press STOP and let the pressure drop naturally.

Top with banana slices and serve.

Peach Quinoa Pudding

(Prep + Cook Time: 20 minutes / Servings: 4)

Ingredients:

2 cups Quinoa
2 Peaches, diced
2 tbsp Raisins
2 cups Milk
2 tsp Peanut Oil
½ tsp Cardamom
2 cups Water
Pinch of Nutmeg
Pinch of Ground Star Anise
2 tbsp Honey

Directions:

Combine all the ingredients except the peaches and honey in the Crock Pot Express.

Close the lid and cook on RICE/RISOTTO for 10 minutes.

Release the pressure naturally. Stir in the peach.

Serve drizzled with honey.

Herbal Yogurt Quinoa Salad

(Prep + Cook Time: 15 minutes / Servings: 2)

Ingredients:

¾ cup Quinoa
2 Green Onions, sliced
6 ounces Yogurt
1 Garlic Clove, minced
2 ½ cups Water
3 tbsp chopped Cilantro
1 tsp chopped Mint
1 tsp chopped Parsley
2 tbsp Oil

Directions:

Heat the oil in your Crock Pot Express on RICE/RISOTTO and cook the onions until soft. Add garlic and cook for 1 more minute. Stir in water and quinoa and close the lid.

Cook for 8 minutes. Allow the pressure to release naturally. Stir in yogurt and herbs.

Pear and Almond Oatmeal

(Prep + Cook Time: 20 minutes / Servings: 4)

Ingredients:

½ cup chopped Almonds
1 ½ cups Oats

1/2 cup Milk
2 ½ cups Water
2 Pears, sliced
1 tbsp Maple Syrup
2 tsp Butter
½ tsp Vanilla
Pinch of Sea Salt

Directions:

Place everything except the pears in your Crock Pot Express.

Cook for 6 minutes on RICE/RISOTTO.

Allow the pressure to release naturally.

Top with pears and serve.

Lemony Oats with Chia Seeds

(Prep + Cook Time: 15 minutes / Servings: 4)

Ingredients:

1 ½ cups Lemon Juice
1 ½ cups Oats
1/3 cup Chia Seeds
3 tbsp Brown Sugar
1 tbsp Honey
Pinch of Salt
1 tbsp Butter
¼ tsp Lemon Zest

Directions:

Melt the butter in your Crock Pot Express on RICE/RISOTTO for 3 minutes.

Stir in the remaining ingredients and close the lid.

Cook for 6 minutes.

Allow the pressure to release naturally.

Quinoa Pilaf with Cherries

(Prep + Cook Time: 20 minutes / Servings: 4)

Ingredients:

1 ½ cups Quinoa
½ cup sliced Almonds
¼ cup chopped Cherries
1 Celery Stalk, chopped
½ Onion, chopped
14 ounces Chicken Broth
¼ cup Water
1 tbsp Butter

Directions:

Melt the butter in the Crock Pot Express on RICE/RISOTTO and cook the onions for 2 minutes.

Add celery and cook for 2 more. Stir in the remaining ingredients. Close the lid and cook for 8 minutes.

Release the pressure naturally and serve.

Mushroom and Parmesan Barley

(Prep + Cook Time: 45 minutes / Servings: 4)

Ingredients:

3 cups Chicken Broth
1 cup Barley
½ cup grated Parmesan Cheese
1 pound Mushrooms, sliced
1 Onion, chopped
3 tbsp Olive Oil
2 tbsp Thyme
1 tsp minced Garlic

Directions:

Heat the oil in your Crock Pot Express on RICE/RISOTTO.

Add the onions and cook for 2 minutes.

Add garlic and cook for 1 more.

Stir in the mushrooms and cook for 4 more minutes.

Stir in the remaining ingredients, except the cheese, and close the lid.

Cook for 8 minutes.

Release the pressure naturally. Stir in the parmesan.

Cheesy Chicken Quinoa

(Prep + Cook Time: 20 minutes / Servings: 4)

Ingredients:

1 ½ cups Quinoa
2 ½ cups Chicken Broth
½ cup shredded Cheddar Cheese
1 cup cooked and shredded Chicken Meat
1 cup Sour Cream
¼ cup grated Parmesan Cheese
Salt and Pepper, to taste

Directions:

Combine the quinoa and broth in Crock Pot Express.

Close the lid and cook on RICE/RISOTTO for 8 minutes.

Allow the pressure to release naturally.

Stir in the remaining ingredients. Cook uncovered for 3 more minutes.

Simple Cornbread

(Prep + Cook Time: 40 minutes / Servings: 4)

Ingredients:

1 ¼ cup Cornmeal
1 cup Buttermilk
½ Butter Stick, melted
2 Eggs, beaten

½ cup Water
½ tsp Salt
1 tsp Baking Powder

Directions:

Combine the dry ingredients in one bowl. Whisk the wet ones in another. Combine the two mixtures gently.

Pour the mixture into a greased baking dish.

Pour water in your Crock Pot Express and lower the trivet.

Place the dish inside and close the lid.

Cook on MEAT/STEW for 30 minutes.

Release the pressure naturally.

Pasta and Rice

Bacon and Cheese Pasta

(Prep + Cook Time: 20 minutes / Servings: 4)

Ingredients:

16 ounces Dry Pasta
1 cup chopped Onions
1 cup diced Bacon
2 ½ cup Tomato Puree
1 tsp Sage
1 tsp Thyme
½ cup grated Cheddar Cheese

Directions:

Cook the bacon in the Crock Pot Express on BEANS/CHILI.

Cook until crispy. Add the onions and cook for a few more minutes.

Stir in the remaining ingredients.

Add enough water to cover.

Close the lid and cook for 8 minutes. Release the pressure naturally.

Stir in the cheddar cheese.

Pasta Bolognese

(Prep + Cook Time: 20 minutes / Servings: 6)

Ingredients:

2 tsp Butter
20 ounces Pasta Noodles
1 1/3 pound mixed Ground Meat
1 ½ pounds Tomato Pasta Sauce
1 tsp Oregano
1 cup chopped Onions
2 tsp minced Garlic

Directions:

Melt the butter in your Crock Pot Express and cook the onions and garlic for 3 minutes. Add meat and cook until browned. Stir in the remaining ingredients

If needed, cover with a little bit of water. Close the lid and cook for 10 minutes on BEANS/CHILI.

Allow the pressure to release naturally.

Spaghetti with Meatballs

(Prep + Cook Time: 30 minutes / Servings: 4)

Ingredients:

10 ounces Noodles
2 Eggs
1 pound Ground Beef
¼ cup Breadcrumbs
2 Eggs
1 jar Spaghetti Sauce
½ tsp minced Garlic

Directions:

Combine the beef, crumbs, garlic, and eggs in a bowl.

Shape the mixture into meatballs.

Combine the sauce and spaghetti in your Crock Pot Express. Add enough water to cover. Add the meatballs and close the lid.

Cook on MEAT/STEW for 14 minutes. Release the pressure naturally.

Chicken Enchilada Pasta

(Prep + Cook Time: 20 minutes / Servings: 6)

Ingredients:

2 Chicken Breasts, diced
3 cups dry Pasta
10 ounces canned Tomatoes
20 ounces canned Enchilada Sauce

1 ¼ cups Water
1 cup diced Onion
1 tsp minced Garlic
1 tsp Taco Seasoning
1 tbsp Oil
2 cups shredded Cheese

Directions:

Heat the oil in your Crock Pot Express on BROWN/SAUTÉ and cook the onions until they become soft.

Stir in the remaining ingredients, except the cheese.

Close the lid and cook for 8 minutes. Release the pressure naturally.

Stir in the cheese and cook uncovered for 2 more minutes.

Noodles with Tuna

(Prep + Cook Time: 20 minutes / Servings: 2)

Ingredients:

8 ounces uncooked Egg Noodles
1 can diced Tomatoes
1 can Tuna Flakes, drained
½ cup chopped Red Onion
1 ¼ cups Water
1 jar marinated and chopped Artichoke
1 tbsp Olive Oil
1 tsp Parsley
1/3 cup crumbled Feta Cheese

Directions:

Heat the oil in the Crock Pot Express on BROWN/SAUTÉ and cook the onions for a few minutes.

Stir in the remaining ingredients, except the cheese.

Close the lid and cook for 4 minutes. Release the pressure naturally. Stir in the feta cheese.

Sausage Penne

(Prep + Cook Time: 20 minutes / Servings: 6)

Ingredients:

18 ounces Penne Pasta
16 ounces Sausage
2 cups Tomato Paste
1 tbsp Olive Oil
2 tsp minced Garlic
1 tsp Oregano
¼ cup grated Parmesan Cheese

Directions:

Heat the oil in the Crock Pot Express.

Add sausage, cook until browned while crumbling.

Add garlic and cook for 1 minute.

Stir in the remaining ingredients, except parmesan, and close the lid.

Cook for 10 minutes on MEAT/STEW.

Release the pressure naturally.

Serve and enjoy.

Chili and Cheesy Beef Pasta

(Prep + Cook Time: 15 minutes / Servings: 6)

Ingredients:

1 pound Ground Beef
2 Scallions, chopped
3 cups cooked Pasta
1 tbsp Butter
½ cup grated Cheddar Cheese
1 tsp minced Garlic
2 cups mild Salsa
½ cup Tomato Puree
1 tbsp Chili Powder

Directions:

Melt the butter in the Crock Pot Express on RICE/RISOTTO. Add scallions and cook for 3 minutes.

Cook the garlic for one minute. Add beef and cook until browned.

Stir in salsa, tomato paste, and spices.

Close the lid and cook for 8 minutes.

Allow the pressure to release naturally and stir in the cheese and pasta.

Cook uncovered for 2 minutes.

Tomato Tuna Pasta Salad

(Prep + Cook Time: 20 minutes / Servings: 6)

Ingredients:

3 Anchovies, chopped
2 cups Tomato Puree
1 cup chopped Tomato
16 ounces dry Pasta
6 cups chopped Lettuce
1 tbsp Olive Oil
1 tsp minced Garlic
2 cans Tuna, drained

Directions:

Heat the oil in the Crock Pot Express and add the anchovies.

Cook for 1 minute. Add garlic and cook for another minute.

Stir in pasta and sauce.

Add some water if needed. It should be enough to cover.

Close the lid and cook on RICE/RISOTTO for 8 minutes.

Release the pressure naturally. Transfer to a bowl.

Stir in the remaining ingredients.

Cheese Tortellini with Broccoli and Turkey

(Prep + Cook Time: 30 minutes / Servings: 6)

Ingredients:

3 Bacon Slices, chopped
1 ½ pounds Turkey Breasts, diced
3 cups Broccoli Florets
8 ounces Cheese Tortellini
¼ cup Heavy Cream
¼ cup Half and Half
2 cups Chicken Stock
1 Onion, chopped
1 Carrot, chopped
1 tbsp chopped Parsley
Salt and Pepper, to taste

Directions:

Cook the bacon in the Crock Pot Express on RICE/RISOTTO until crispy. Add onions and garlic and cook for 2 minutes Add turkey and cook until no longer pink.

Stir in the remaining ingredients, except heavy cream.

Cook for 7 minutes. Release the pressure naturally. Stir in the heavy cream.

Pizza Pasta

(Prep + Cook Time: 30 minutes / Servings: 6)

Ingredients:

1 pound Pasta
16 ounces Pasta Sauce
8 ounces Pizza Sauce
1 pound Italian Sausage
20 ounces Pepperoni
8 ounces shredded Mozzarella Cheese
3 ½ cups Water
1 tbsp Butter
1 tsp minced Garlic

Directions:

Heat the oil in the Crock Pot Express on RICE/RISOTTO.

Cook the sausage and garlic for a few minutes.

Stir in the remaining ingredients, except the cheese and half of the pepperoni.

Close the lid and cook for 8 minutes.

Allow the pressure to release naturally.

Stir in the cheese and pepperoni.

Colorful Risotto

(Prep + Cook Time: 40 minutes / Servings: 6)

Ingredients:

2 cups Brown Rice
4 cups Veggie Broth
½ cup chopped Carrots
1 Yellow Bell Pepper, chopped
1 Green Bell Pepper, chopped
2 Tomatoes, chopped
1 Red Onion, chopped
3 tsp Oil
1 cups Peas
Salt and Pepper, to taste

Directions:

Heat the oil in your Crock Pot Express on RICE/RISOTTO.

Add the onions and cook for a few minutes.

Add carrots and peppers and cook for 2 more minutes.

Stir in the remaining ingredients.

Close the lid and cook for 20 minutes.

Release the pressure naturally.

Rice Pilaf with Chicken

(Prep + Cook Time: 40 minutes / Servings: 8)

Ingredients:

2 cups Rice
2 Chicken Breasts, diced
1 tsp minced Garlic
1 Onion, chopped
2 Bell Peppers, chopped
1 tbsp Oil
4 cups Chicken Broth
1 tsp Rosemary
Salt and Pepper, to taste

Directions:

Heat the oil in your Cooking Pot on RICE/RISOTTO.

Cook the onions for 2 minutes. Add garlic and cook for 1 more minute. Add peppers and cook for 2 minutes.

Stir in the remaining ingredients. Close the lid and cook for 25 minutes. Release the pressure naturally.

Apple and Apricot Wild Rice

(Prep + Cook Time: 30 minutes / Servings: 8)

Ingredients:

2 cups Wild Rice
1/3 cup Maple Syrup
½ cup dried Apricots, chopped
1 ½ cups Apple Juice
½ cup Milk
3 Egg Yolks
¼ tsp ground Ginger
½ tsp Cinnamon
Pinch of Salt
4 cups Water

Directions:

Combine everything, except the apricots, in your Cooking Pot. Cook on RICE/ RISOTTO for 25 minutes.

Release the pressure naturally and stir in the apricots.

Fennel Jasmine Rice

(Prep + Cook Time: 15 minutes / Servings: 4)

Ingredients:

1 ½ cups Jasmine Rice
1 cup Fennel Bulb, chopped
2 Spring Onions, chopped
1 cup chopped Parsnips
1 Carrot, chopped
2 cups Chicken Stock
1 cup Water
1 tsp Sage
1 tbsp Oil
Salt and Pepper, to taste

Directions:

Heat the oil in your Cooking Pot on RICE/RISOTTO. Cook the onions until soft.

Add parsnips, carrots, and fennel and cook for 2 more minutes. Stir in the remaining ingredients.

Close the lid and cook for 10 minutes. Release the pressure naturally.

Shrimp Risotto

(Prep + Cook Time: 20 minutes / Servings: 4)

Ingredients:

1 pound Shrimp, peeled and deveined
1 ½ cups White Rice
1 tbsp Oil
3 tbsp Butter

3 cups Fish Stock
2 tsp minced Garlic
2 Shallots, chopped
¼ cup White Wine
Salt and Pepper, to taste

Directions:

Heat the oil and melt the butter in the Express Crock on RICE/RISOTTO. Cook the onion and garlic for 3 minutes.

Add shrimp and cook for 3 minutes.

Stir in the remaining ingredients and close the lid. Cook for 8 minutes. Release the pressure naturally.

Spinach Vermouth Risotto

(Prep + Cook Time: 20 minutes / Servings: 4)

Ingredients:

1 cup sliced Mushrooms
2 cups chopped Spinach
½ cup Vermouth
1 cup Rice
1 Zucchini, sliced
½ cup Parmesan Cheese
1 Shallot, chopped
1 tsp minced Garlic
1 tbsp Oil
2 cups Chicken Stock

Directions:

Heat the oil in your Cooking Pot to RICE/RISOTTO.

Cook the shallot and garlic for 2 minutes. Add mushrooms and cook for 3 more minutes.

Stir in the remaining ingredients, except the cheese, and close the lid. Cook for 8 minutes. Release the pressure naturally. Stir in the cheese.

Chicken and Rice Salad

(Prep + Cook Time: 15 minutes / Servings: 4)

Ingredients:

2 cups Brown Rice
2 Celery Stalks, chopped
1 cup diced Carrots
2 ½ cups Stock
½ pound Chicken Breasts, diced
2 cups Water
3 Spring Onions, sliced

Dressing:

2 tbsp melted Butter
4 tbsp Mayonnaise
2 tbsp chopped Chives
1 tsp Mustard
1/3 cup Olive Oil
Salt and Pepper, to taste

Directions:

Combine all the salad ingredients and close the lid.

Cook on RICE/RISOTTO for 10 minutes.

Release the pressure naturally and transfer to a bowl.

Whisk together the dressing ingredients and drizzle over the salad.

Lemony Rice with Veggies

(Prep + Cook Time: 15 minutes / Servings: 8)

Ingredients:

1 cup Rice
½ cup chopped Onions
1 cup Broccoli Florets, frozen
1 cup sliced Carrots
1 cup Peas

1 tbsp Oil
2 tsp Lemon Zest
¼ cup Lemon Juice
2 cups Veggie Stock

Directions:

Heat the oil in your Express Crock Pot on RICE/RISOTTO.

Cook the onions for 2 minutes.

Stir the remaining ingredients and cook for 10 minutes.

Release the pressure naturally.

Coconut Rice

(Prep + Cook Time: 10 minutes / Servings: 6)

Ingredients:

1 ½ cup Rice
¼ cup toasted Coconut
14 ounces Coconut Milk
¼ tsp Sugar
Pinch of Salt

Directions:

Place all the ingredients in your Cooking Pot and close the lid. Cook on RICE/ RISOTTO for 7 minutes.

Release the pressure naturally.

Simple Mushroom Risotto

(Prep + Cook Time: 15 minutes / Servings: 4)

Ingredients:

1 ½ cups Arborio Rice
½ cup dried Chanterelle Mushrooms, soaked, drained, chopped
½ cup grated Parmesan Cheese
¼ cup chopped Onion
1 tsp minced Garlic

4 cups Chicken Stock
1 ½ cups Water
1 tbsp Butter
¼ tsp Salt
¼ tsp White Pepper

Directions:

Melt the butter in the Crock Pot Express and cook the onion and garlic for 2 minutes.

Place the remaining ingredients.

Close the lid and cook for 10 minutes on RICE/RISOTTO.

Release the pressure naturally.

Soups

Creamy Pumpkin Soup

(Prep + Cook Time: 55 minutes / Servings: 3)

Ingredients:

1 cup Pumpkin puree
2 cups Chicken broth
2 Garlic cloves
1 cup heavy Cream
2 tablespoons Olive oil
Salt and black pepper, to taste

Directions:

In the Crock Pot Express, add all ingredients and cook on SOUP mode for 45 minutes.

Transfer to a blender and blend well. Pour into bowls and serve warm.

Spinach Soup

(Prep + Cook Time: 35 minutes / Servings: 4)

Ingredients:

4 cups Vegetable broth
1 cup Baby Spinach
2 Garlic cloves, minced
½ cup Milk
2 tablespoons Olive oil
1 cup Heavy cream
1 bunch Coriander, puree
½ teaspoon Chili flakes
¼ teaspoon Salt

Directions:

Heat oil and add garlic cloves, cook for 1 minute on BROWN/SAUTÉ mode.

Add vegetable broth, spinach, coriander puree, cream, chili flake, and salt, mix well. Cook on SOUP mode for 30 minutes.

Pour in milk and cook for 5 minutes on low heat. Spoon into serving bowls.

Chicken Broth with Broccoli

(Prep + Cook Time: 25 minutes / Servings: 4)

Ingredients:

1 package Broccoli, frozen
4 cups Chicken broth
½ cup Butter
1 Onion, chopped
1 tbsp. Garlic powder
½ cup Cornstarch
1 cup Water

Directions:

Add butter and onion into the Cooking pot. Press SAUTÉ and stir-fry for a minute.

Add in the cornstarch, water, garlic powder, broccoli and chicken broth. Press SOUP on HIGH pressure for 45 minutes.

When ready, strain the stock. Transfer the stock into containers and freeze up to 2 months.

Turkey Mixed Soup Recipe

(Prep + Cook Time: 30 minutes / Servings: 4)

Ingredients:

3 cups Turkey breast, cubed
4 cups Chicken broth
4 stalks Celery, chopped
2 Garlic cloves
1 Onion, chopped
2 cups Green onions, chopped
Salt and pepper, to taste

Directions:

Add all ingredients to the Cooking Pot and stir well. Cook it on SOUP on High pressure for 30 minutes.

Once complete, and the pressure released, set aside to cool for 15-20 minutes before serving.

Mushroom Soup Recipe

(Prep + Cook Time: 40 minutes / Servings: 4)

Ingredients:

4 cups Chicken stock
4 cups Mushrooms, chopped
2 cups Parmesan, shredded
2 tbsp. Butter
2 Onions, chopped
2 tbsp. Flour
2 Garlic cloves
1 cup Thyme, chopped

Directions:

Heat butter and add in the onions into the Cooking pot and stir-fry on SAUTÉ mode for 1 minute. Add in mushrooms, garlic cloves, thyme, and chicken stock. Stir well to combine.

Close the lid and select SOUP on HIGH pressure for 25 minutes. Once ready, open the lid and add the flout, let simmer for 15 minutes on SLOW cook mode.

Once ready, sprinkle with shredded cheese and serve!

Black Beans Soup

(Prep + Cook Time: 30 minutes / Servings: 4)

Ingredients:

4 cups Black Beans
4 cups Water
2 small Onions, chopped

2 tbsp. Olive oil
1 tbsp. Chili powder
1 tbsp. Oregano
½ cup Green chilies
Cilantro leaves to garnish
Salt to taste

Directions:

Pour in the oil into the Crock Pot Express and SAUTÉ it.

Add in the onions, oregano, green chilies, chili powder, black beans, and salt. Stir well.

Cook on SOUP on HIGH pressure for 25 minutes. Allow the pressure to realease naturally.

Chicken Noodle Soup

(Prep + Cook Time: 30 minutes / Servings: 4)

Ingredients:

1 lb. Chicken breast, cubed
1 package of Noodles
1 lb. Bok Choy
4 cups Chicken stock
3 cups hot Water
2 Carrots
Salt to taste
Cilantro or Parsley

Directions:

Add all ingredients in the Cooking pot. Seal the lid and press SOUP. Cook on HIGH pressure for 30 minutes.

Once ready, allow for a natural pressure release.

Sprinkle with cilantro or parsley and serve.

Sweet Potato Soup

(Prep + Cook Time: 45 minutes / Servings: 4)

Ingredients:

4 cups Chicken broth
3 Sweet Potatoes, peeled and diced
2 tbsp. Butter
1 Onion, chopped
1 cup Sweet corn kernels
1 tbsp. Cornstarch
Salt and pepper, to taste

Directions:

Add butter and onion into the Cooking pot. Stir-fry for 1 minute on BROWN/ SAUTÉ Add in the chicken broth and stir well. Cook for 2 minutes.

Add in sweet potatoes, corn, salt and pepper, and cornstarch.

Press SOUP, set ot HIGH pressure for 40 minutes.

Chicken and Kale Soup

(Prep + Cook Time: 30 minutes / Servings: 4)

Ingredients:

1 lb. Chicken thighs, cubed
2 Tomatoes, diced
2 Potatoes, peeled and diced
3 cups Chicken broth
2 cups Kale, chopped
2 tbsp. Olive oil
Salt and pepper

Directions:

Heat oil in the Crock Pot Express on BROWN/SAUTÉ mode.

Add in chicken broth, potatoes, tomatoes, kale, chicken cubes, salt and pepper.

Press SOUP and cook on HIGH pressure for 25 minutes.

Once ready, serve inmediately.

Vegetable Soup

(Prep + Cook Time: 30 minutes / Servings: 4)

Ingredients:

1 cup Broccoli florets
1 Red Bell Pepper, sliced
1 Green Bell Pepper, sliced
3 cups Vegetable broth
1 Carrot, sliced
1 Onion, sliced
2 Garlic cloves, minced
1 tablespoon Lemon juice
½ teaspoon Black pepper
¼ teaspoon Salt
1 tablespoon Cooking oil

Directions:

Set the Crock Pot Express on BROWN/SAUTÉ mode.

Heat oil, add onion and garlic cloves, and stir-fry for 1 minute. Add in all the vegetables, stir-fry and cook for 8-10 minutes.

Add in the vegetable broth, salt, and pepper and mix well.

Close the lid and press SOUP on HIGH pressure for 25 minutes.

Once ready, drizzle lemon juice and ladle into serving bowls.

Bell Pepper and Cabbage Soup

(Prep + Cook Time: 60 minutes / Servings: 4)

Ingredients:

4 cups Chicken broth
1 red Bell pepper, sliced
1 cup Cabbage, shredded
1 Onion, sliced
1 tablespoon Fish sauce
2 Garlic cloves, minced
½ teaspoon Black pepper

¼ teaspoon Salt
1 tablespoon Oil

Directions:

Heat oil in the Crock Pot Express, and add onion.

Cook for 1 minute on Sauté mode.

Add the garlic, bell pepper, and cabbage and cook for 6 more minutes.

Add chicken broth, fish sauce, salt, and pepper and mix well.

Seal the lid and press SOUP.

Cook on high pressure for 30 minutes.

Ladle into serving bowls and enjoy.

Slow-Cooked Yellow Lentils Soup

(Prep + Cook Time: 75 minutes / Servings: 4)

Ingredients:

1 cup Yellow lentils, soaked
2 cups Water
3 cups Chicken broth
¼ teaspoon Turmeric powder
½ teaspoon Ginger paste
1 Onion, chopped
2 tablespoons Butter
2 Garlic cloves, minced
½ teaspoon Chili powder
¼ teaspoon Salt

Directions:

Place all ingredients in the Crock Pot Express, and stir well.

Set the Pot on SLOW cook mode and cook for 75 minutes.

Pour the soup into bowls and serve.

Desserts

Chocolate Cake

(Prep + Cook Time: 45 minutes / Servings: 10)

Ingredients:

2 1/2 cups Yogurt
2 1/2 cups of all-purpose Flour
1 1/2 cups of Granulated Sugar
1 cup of Oil
2 teaspoons of Baking soda
3 tablespoons Cocoa, unsweetened
For the glaze:
7 ounces Dark Chocolate
1/2 cup Sugar
1/2 cup Milk
4 ounces Butter, unsalted

Directions:

In a large bowl, combine yogurt, flour, sugar, oil, baking soda, and cocoa.

Beat well with an electric mixer.

Transfer the mixture to a large springform pan.

Wrap the pan in foil and place in your Crock Pot Express.

Seal the lid and set the steam release handle.

Press the "MULTIGRAIN" button and set the timer to 35 minutes.

Remove the springform pan and unwrap. Let cool.

Meanwhile, melt the chocolate in a microwave.

Transfer to a medium-sized bowl and whisk in the butter, milk, and sugar.

Beat with an electric mixer and pour the mixture over the cake.

Refrigerate for at several hours before serving.

Simple Fig Dessert

(Prep + Cook Time: 35 minutes / Servings: 6)

Ingredients:

1 1/2 pounds fresh figs
1/2 pound sugar
2 tablespoons lemon zest
8 cups water
1 tespoon ground nutmeg

Directions:

Place all ingredients and stir well.

Close the lid and press DESSERT, set pressure to LOW, and time to 20 minutes.

Press the START/STOP button and remove the figs.

Set your Crock Pot Express on BRONW/SAUTÉ mode, on HIGH and cook until the sauce is reduced by half. Serve figs with the sauce and yogurt/cream.

Pumpkin Pudding

(Prep + Cook Time: 30 minutes / Servings: 4)

Ingredients:

1 lb Pumpkin, peeled and chopped into bite-sized pieces
1 cup Granulated Sugar
½ cup Cornstarch
4 cups Pumpkin juice, unsweetened
3 Cloves
1 tsp Cinnamon, ground

Directions:

Place the pumpking in the Cooking Pot.

In another bowl, combine sugar with pumpkin juice. Mix well until sugar dissolves completely.

Now pour the mixture into the Multi-cooker and stir in one cup of cornstarch. Add cinnamon, cloves, and give it a good stir.

Close the lid and press BEANS/CHILI button. Set the timer for 10 minutes.

Once ready, open the cooker and pour the pudding into 4 serving bowls.

Cool to a room temperature and then place into the refrigerator. Chill overnight.

Vanilla Cake

(Prep + Cook Time: 20 minutes / Servings: 7-8)

Ingredients:

3 standard Cake crusts
4 cups Milk
½ cup Vanilla pudding powder
¼ cup Granulated sugar
10.5 ounces box Chocolate chips
¼ cup Walnuts, minced

Directions:

Set the Crock Pot Express on BROWN/SAUTÉ mode. Combine the vanilla pudding powder with sugar and milk. Cook until the pudding thickens, stirring constantly. Remove from the pot.

Place one crust at the bottom of your springform pan. Pour half of the pudding and sprinkle with minced walnuts and chocolate chips. Cover with another crust and repeat the process. Finish with the final crust and wrap in foil.

Place springform pan in your Cooking pot and seal the lid. Press BEANS/CHILI button and set on HIGH pressure for 5 minutes.

Remove the cake and chill to a room temperature. Refrigerate overnight.

Blueberry Pancakes

(Prep + Cook Time: 25 minutes / Servings: 4)

Ingredients:

1 cup Buckwheat flour
1 Egg
2 teaspoon Baking powder
1 1/2 cups skim Milk
1/2 teaspoon Salt

1 teaspoon Vanilla sugar
1 cup Greek yogurt
1 cup fresh Blueberries

Directions:

In a medium-sized mixing bowl, combine milk and egg. Beat well with a whisking attachment on high - until foamy. Gradually add flour and keep beating until combined.

Add baking powder, vanilla sugar and salt. Continue to beat on high for 4 more minutes.

Plug in your Cooker pot and grease with oil. Spoon 3 tablespoons of batter into the pot. Close the lid and press BEANS/CHILI on low pressure. Cook for 10 minutes.

Open the lid and repeat the process with the remaining batter.

Top the pancakes with Greek yogurt and blueberries.

Egg Cake

(Prep + Cook Time: 25 minutes / Servings: 4)

Ingredients:

3 tbsp. Milk
3 tbsp. Sugar
3 egg Yolks
2 cups Chocolate chips
3 egg Whites
2 cups Flour

Directions:

Add the first 2 ingredients in a bowl and mix well. Stir in the remaining ingredients and mix well to combine.

Pour the batter into a round baking tray.

Place the baking tray in the Crock Pot Express and cook on DESSERT for 20 minutes.

Once ready, serve warm!

Date Toffee Dessert

(Prep + Cook Time: 50 minutes / Servings: 5)

Ingredients:

1 cup Dates, chopped
1 Egg
1 cup Flour
1/2 cup boiling Water
1/2 cup brown Sugar
2 cups Water
1 tablespoon Blackstrap molasses
1/2 tespoon Vanilla extract
1/2 tespoon Baking powder
1/2 tespoon Salt

Directions:

Mix the sugar and butter until fluffy. Combine the dry ingredients in one bowl.

In another bowl, combine boiling water, dates, and molasses.

Mix gradually the date mixture and the dry ingredients into the butter mixture.

Grease 5 ramekins and fill each one of them with the mixture.

Pour the water into your Cooking Pot, and place the ramekins on the rack.

Close the lid, select BEANS/CHILI, and cook on HIGH for 30 minutes.

Easy Apple Pie

(Prep + Cook Time: 45 minutes / Servings: 5)

Ingredients:

Pie dough
1 1/2 pounds Apples, peeled and cut into pieces
1 Egg, beaten, for brushing
1/2 cup Granulated sugar
1/2 cup Breadcrumbs
1 tbsp. Vanilla sugar
1/2 cup oil
1/2 cup all-purpose flour
2 teaspoons cinnamon

Directions:

In a bowl, combine the apples, breadcrumbs, vanilla sugar, granulated sugar, and cinnamon. Set aside.

Sprinkle flour on a surface and roll out the pie dough making 2 circle-shaped crusts.

Grease the Express Crock with oil and place inside 1 piecrust. Top with apple mixture and cover with the other circle-shaped crust.

Crimp the edges to complete the seal, and brush with egg.

Sprinkle the pie with powdered sugar. Close the lid, and seal the steam valve.

Press BEANS/CHILI and cook for 20 minutes. Release the steam naturally.

Easy Apple Pie

(Prep + Cook Time: 15 minutes / Servings: 5)

Ingredients:

7 Egg yolks
4 cups of Heavy Cream
1 Vanilla Bean, split lengthwise
1 1/2 cups Sugar
1/2 tespoon Salt

Directions:

In a large bowl, combine the egg yolks, heavy cream and 1 cup of sugar. Mix with electric mixer.

Scrape the seeds out of the vanilla bean and add them to the mixture along with the salt. Mix again.

Pour the mixture into 5 ramekins and set aside.

Take 3x11 inches long pieces of aluminum foil, and roll them up into snake-shaped pieces.

Curl into a circles, pinching the ends together.

Place at the bottom of the Crock Pot Express.

Place each ramekin on aluminum circle, and pour water to cover 1/3 of the way.

Press BEANS/CHILI and cook on HIGH pressure for 10 minutes.

Allow for a natural pressure release.

Remove the ramekins from the Cooking Pot, and add one 1 tbsp. of sugar in each ramekin.

Burn the surface with a culinary torch until lightly brown.

Allow to cool and serve.

"Express" Brownies

(Prep + Cook Time: 40 minutes / Servings: 4)

Ingredients:

2 Eggs
1/2 cup Butter, melted
1/4 teaspoon Salt
1 cup Sugar
1/4 cup Cocoa powder
1 cup Flour
1 teaspoon Baking powder
1 teaspoon Honey
2 cups Water

Directions:

Pour the water into your Coooking Pot.

Mix all ingredients in a bowl. Stir well to combine.

Grease a pan with cooking spray. Pour the batter inside it.

Place it in your Crock Pot Exprees, and close the lid.

Press BEANS/CHILI, and cook on HIGH pressure for 35 minutes.

Chef's Selection

Chicken Liver Pate

(Prep + Cook Time: 15 minutes / Servings: 16)

Ingredients:

1 pound Chicken Livers
1 cup chopped Leek
1/3 cup Rum
2 tsp Olive Oil
2 tbsp Butter
1 tbsp Sage
1 tsp Basil
1 tsp Thyme
3 Anchovies

Directions:

Heat the oil in your Crock Pot Express on POULTRY and cook the leeks for a few minutes. Add the liver and cook for 3 minutes.

Stir in the rum and close the lid. Cook for 10 minutes.

Release the pressure naturally. Stir in the remaining ingredients. Transfer to a food processor and pulse until smooth.

Colby and Pancetta Frittata

(Prep + Cook Time: 25 minutes / Servings: 4)

Ingredients:

6 Eggs, beaten
½ cup grated Colby Cheese
6 Pancetta Slices, cooked and crumbled
3 tbsp Sour Cream
½ tsp Onion Powder
2 tsp Butter, melted
¼ tsp Pepper
1 ½ cups Water

Directions:

Pour the water in your Crock Pot Express and lower the trivet.

Whisk the remaining ingredients in a baking dish.

Place the dish in the Crock Pot Express and close the lid.

Cook on POULTRY for 15 minutes.

Release the pressure naturally.

Eggs de Provence

(Prep + Cook Time: 20 minutes / Servings: 4)

Ingredients:

8 Eggs
1 cup Heavy Cream
2 Shallots, chopped
1 ¼ cups Bacon de Provence, cooked and crumbled
1 ½ cups chopped Kale
1 tbsp mixed Herbs by choice
Salt and Pepper, to taste
4 tbsp Water

Directions:

Whisk the eggs with the water and cream in a baking dish.

Stir in the shallots, bacon, kale, and herbs.

Season with salt and pepper.

Cover with a piece of foil.

Pour 1 ½ cups of water in the Crock Pot Express and lower the trivet.

Place the dish inside.

Close the lid and cook on RICE/RISOTTO for 18 minutes.

Release the pressure naturally.

Pineapple and Honey Risotto

(Prep + Cook Time: 15 minutes / Servings: 6)

Ingredients:

2 cups White Rice
½ cup Honey
1 cup Orange Juice
1 cup crushed Pineapple
1/3 cup Water
2 tbsp Ghee
½ tsp Vanilla

Directions:

Place the rice, juice, water, ghee, and vanilla in your Crock Pot Express.

Close the lid and cook for 6 minutes on RICE/RISOTTO.

Release the pressure naturally. Stir in the pineapple and drizzle with honey.

Squid and Peas

(Prep + Cook Time: 30 minutes / Servings: 4)

Ingredients:

1 pound Squid, cleaned and chopped
1 pound Peas
1 Onion, chopped
½ pound canned Tomatoes
1 tbsp White Wine
Salt and Pepper, to taste

Directions:

Coat the Crock Pot Express with cooking spray and cook the onions for 3 minutes.

Add squid and cook for another 3 minutes.

Stir in the remaining ingredients and add some water, enough to cover everything.

Close the lid and cook on STEAM for 20 minutes. Release the pressure naturally.

Whole Hog Omelet

(Prep + Cook Time: 40 minutes / Servings: 4)

Ingredients:

6 Eggs, beaten
1 cup shredded Cheddar Cheese
½ cup diced Ham
1 cup ground Sausage
4 Bacon Slices, cooked and crumbled
½ cup Milk
2 Green Onions, chopped
Salt and Pepper, to taste

Directions:

Whisk all the ingredients together. Transfer to a baking dish.

Pour 1 ½ cups water in your Crock Pot Express and lower the trivet.

Place the dish inside the cooker.

Close the lid and cook for 20 minutes on POULTRY.

Release the pressure naturally and serve.

Farmer's Meal

(Prep + Cook Time: 20 minutes / Servings: 8)

Ingredients:

½ cup Barley
½ pound cooked Ham, chopped
1 cup sliced Mushrooms
1 cup chopped Bell Peppers
2 tbsp Butter
2 Green Onions, chopped
2 cups Veggie Stock
1 tsp minced Ginger
¼ cup chopped Celery
Salt and Pepper, to taste

Directions:

Melt the butter in the Crock Pot Express.

Add the onions and cook for 3 minutes.

Add mushrooms, celery, and bell peppers and cook for 3 more minutes. Add ham and ginger and cook for 1 minute.

Stir in the remaining ingredients. Close the lid and cook on RICE/RISOTTO for 10 minutes. Release the pressure naturally.

Coq Au Vin

(Prep + Cook Time: 60 minutes / Servings: 4)

Ingredients:

2 pounds Chicken Breasts
4 ounces Bacon chopped
14 ounces Red Wine
1 cup chopped Parsley
2 Onions, chopped
12 small Potatoes, halved
7 ounces White Mushrooms, sliced
1 tsp Garlic Paste
2 tbsp Flour
¼ cup Oil
2 tbsp Cognac
Salt and Pepper, to taste

Directions:

Heat the oil in the Crock Pot Express on BROWN/SAUTÉ and brown the chicken on all sides.

Stir in onion and bacon and cook for 2 minutes.

Add garlic and cook for 1 minute. Whisk in the flour and cognac. Stir in the remaining ingredients, except the mushrooms, and close the lid.

Press STOP and choose MEAT/STEW. Cook for 30 minutes. Release the pressure naturally.

Stir in the mushrooms and cook for 15 more minutes.

Glazed Orange Salmon

(Prep + Cook Time: 25 minutes / Servings: 4)

Ingredients:

4 Salmon Filets
2 tsp Orange Zest
3 tbsp Orange Juice
1 tbsp Olive Oil
1 tsp minced Ginger
1 cup White Wine
Salt and Pepper, to taste

Directions:

Place everything except the salmon in the Crock Pot Express. Whisk to combine.

Add salmon and close the lid. Cook on STEAM and cook for 7 minutes. Release the pressure naturally and serve.

Veal and Mushrooms

(Prep + Cook Time: 45 minutes / Servings: 4)

Ingredients:

2 pounds Veal Shoulder, cut into chunks
16 ounces Shallots, chopped
16 ounces Potatoes, chopped
10 ounces Beef Stock
8 ounces Mushrooms, sliced
3 ½ tbsp Olive Oil
2 tbsp Chives, chopped
2 ounces White Wine
1 tsp minced Garlic
1 tbsp Flour
1 tsp Sage

Directions:

Heat 1 ½ tbsp oil in your Crock Pot Express. Add veal and coat with flour. Cook until browned.

Add the rest of the oil and cook the mushrooms for 3 minutes.

Add onions and garlic and cook for 2 minutes.

Stir in the wine, stock, and sage.

Close the lid and cook on MEAT/STEW for 20 minutes.

Release the pressure naturally.

Ziti Pork Meatballs

(Prep + Cook Time: 25 minutes / Servings: 4)

Ingredients:

¾ pound ground Pork
1 box Ziti
2 Tomatoes, chopped
1 cup Veggie Stock
3 tsp Oil
2 cups Cauliflower Florets
2 Bell Peppers, chopped
1/3 cup Cider
1/3 cup Water
1 Red Onion, chopped
½ tbsp Basil

Directions:

Combine the pork and basil and shape this mixture into meatballs.

Heat the oil in your Crock Pot Express on MEAT/STEW and cook the meatballs until browned.

Set aside.

Cook the onions, cauliflowers, and peppers for a few minutes.

Stir in the remaining ingredients, including the meatballs.

Close the lid and cook for 15 minutes.

Release the pressure naturally and serve.

Cheese and Prosciutto Eggs

(Prep + Cook Time: 10 minutes / Servings: 4)

Ingredients:

8 Eggs
8 Prosciutto Slices
4 Swiss Cheese Slices
4 tbsp chopped Spring Onions
2 tbsp chopped Parsley
2 tbsp Butter

Directions:

Pour 1 ½ cups water in your Crock Pot Express and lower the trivet.

Coat 4 ramekins with the butter.

Break 2 eggs into each ramekin and top with the spring onions.

Place 2 prosciutto slice over the onions and top with ½ slice of cheese.

Sprinkle the parsley over.

Cover the ramekins with foil and place them in the Crock Pot Express.

Close the lid and cook for 6 minutes on RICE/RISOTTO.

Release the pressure naturally.

Easy Duck with Cucumbers and Ginger

(Prep + Cook Time: 50 minutes / Servings: 8)

Ingredients:

1 Duck, chopped into pieces
1 Cucumber, chopped
2 Carrots, chopped
1-inch Ginger, chopped
1 tbsp White Wine
2 cups Water
Salt and Pepper, to taste

Directions:

Place all of the ingredients in your Crock Pot Express.

Season with salt and pepper to taste.

Close the lid and cook on POULTRY for 40 minutes.

Release the pressure for 5 minutes.

Buttery and Lemony Dill Clams

(Prep + Cook Time: 10 minutes / Servings: 4)

Ingredients:

28 scrubbed Clams
1 tbsp minced Dill
¼ cup Water
½ cup White Wine
3 tbsp Lemon Juice
2 tbsp Brown Sugar
1 tsp minced Garlic

Directions:

Combine all of the ingredients in the Crock Pot Express and add the clams inside. Close the lid and cook on MEAT/STEW for 5 minutes.

Release the pressure naturally.

Pork Liver and Spring Onion Pate

(Prep + Cook Time: 25 minutes / Servings: 10)

Ingredients:

1 pound Pork Liver, chopped
4 Spring Onions, chopped
2 Tomatoes, chopped
2 tbsp Oil
4 Garlic Cloves, sliced
3 tbsp Flour
1 tsp Basil
Salt and Pepper, to taste

Directions:

Heat the oil in your Crock Pot Express on RICE/RISOTTO.

Brown the liver for about 3 minutes.

Stir in the remaining ingredients and cook for another minute.

Pour a little bit of water to cover.

Close the lid and cook for 15 minutes.

Release the pressure naturally.

Transfer the mixture to a food processor and pulse until smooth.

Serve with crusty bread and enjoy!

Party and Holidays

Biscuits, Pork, and Gravy

(Prep + Cook Time: 30 minutes / Servings: 8)

Ingredients:

1 ½ pounds ground Pork
8 Biscuits
¾ cup Apple Cider
1 1/3 cups Milk
½ cup Flour
3 tsp Butter
½ cup chopped Onions
1 tsp minced Garlic
1 tsp Thyme
1 tsp Rosemary
Salt and Pepper, to taste

Directions:

Melt the butter in your EXPRESS CROCK on BEANS/CHILI. Add the pork and cook until browned.

Add onions and garlic and cook for another 1-2 minutes.

Stir in the cider, thyme, and rosemary. Close the lid and cook for 15 minutes. Release the pressure naturally.

Whisk together the flour and milk and pour over the pork.

Close the lid and cook on BEANS/CHILI for 5 minutes.

Serve over biscuits and enjoy!

Pork Shoulder with Pineapple and Pomegranate

(Prep + Cook Time: 50 minutes / Servings: 8)

Ingredients:

3-pound Pork Shoulder
8 Garlic Cloves, smashed

1 Onion, diced
3 tbsp Chile Powder
1 cup Pomegranate Juice
1 cup Pineapple Juice
2 cups Chicken Stock
1 cup diced Pineapple
1 tbsp Cumin
1 tbsp Salt
1 tsp Pepper
1/3 cu Pomegranate Seeds

Directions:

Rub the spices in the pork and place it in the Crock Pot Express. Combine the remaining ingredients, except the molasses, in a bowl.

Coat the Crock Pot Express with cooking spray and sear the pork on MEAT/STEW on all sides. Pour the pineapple mixture over.

Close the lid and cook for 30 minutes. Release the pressure naturally. Serve topped with the cooking liquid and sprinkled with pomegranate seeds.

Sugary Ham

(Prep + Cook Time: 80 minutes / Servings: 4)

Ingredients:

3-pound Ham
1 cup Brown Sugar
1 ½ tbsp ground Mustard
Water
Vinegar

Directions:

Slice your ham into serving portions, but not all the way through. Place it in the Cooking Pot.

Make a mixture of water to vinegar with a ratio of 2:1 and pour over the ham. Make sure to have enough liquid, but be careful not to exceed the limit line.

Close the lid and cook for 35 minutes on MEAT/STEW.

Combine the mustard and brown sugar and sprinkle all over the ham.

Close the lid again and cook for another half an hour.

Release the pressure naturally.

Vegan Holiday Roast

(Prep + Cook Time: 20 minutes / Servings: 8)

Ingredients:

1 Field Roast (such as Hazelnut Cranberry Roast En Croute)
1 cup Vegetable Broth
1 Celery Stalk, chopped
1 Onion, diced
2 tsp minced Garlic
Salt and Pepper, to taste
1 ½ tbsp Olive Oil

Directions:

Heat the oil in your Crock Pot Express and cook the onions and celery until soft. Add garlic and cook for one more minute.

Add roast and broth and season with salt and pepper. Close the lid and cook for 10 minutes. Release the pressure naturally and serve.

Hassle-Free Holiday Roast

(Prep + Cook Time: 75 minutes / Servings: 8)

Ingredients:

3 pounds Beef Roast
2 cups Beef Broth
1 cup chopped Onions
2 tsp Olive Oil
Salt and Pepper, to taste

Directions:

Season the meat with salt and pepper.

Heat the oil in your Crock Pot Express on BROWN/SAUTÉ. Add garlic and cook until soft. Add roast and sear on all sides.

Pour the broth over and close the lid. Cook for 3 hours on SLOW cook mode.

Apple and Squash Mash

(Prep + Cook Time: 15 minutes / Servings: 6)

Ingredients:

1 ½ pounds Butternut Squash, cubed
2 Apples, peeled and diced
2 tbsp Butter
1 Onion, chopped
¼ cup Milk
Pinch of Powdered Ginger
Pinch of Nutmeg
Pinch of Cinnamon
¼ tsp Salt

Directions:

Pour 1 ½ water in the Crock Pot Express.

Add the squash, onion, and apple in the steaming basket in the Crock Pot Express.

Close the lid and cook on MEAT/STEW for 10 minutes.

Allow the pressure to release naturally. Transfer to a bowl and add the remaining ingredients. Mash with a potato masher.

Quail and Pancetta

(Prep + Cook Time: 25 minutes / Servings: 4)

Ingredients:

2 Quails, cleaned
½ cup Champagne
4 Carrots, chopped
4 ounces Pancetta, chopped

2 Scallions, chopped
½ Fennel Bulb, chopped
1 tsp Thyme
1 tsp Rosemary
Juice of 1 Lemon
1 tbsp Olive Oil
Salt and Pepper, to taste

Directions:

Add the fennel and carrot in the Crock Pot Express and add 2 cups of water. Cook on MEAT/STEW for 2 minutes.

Transfer to a plate and reserve the broth.

Heat the oil in the Crock Pot Express and cook the scallions, pancetta, and all the herbs. Add the quail and brown on all sides.

Pour the broth and champagne over. Close the lid and cook for 10 minutes. Serve with the carrots and fennel.

White Wine Mussels

(Prep + Cook Time: 15 minutes / Servings: 4)

Ingredients:

1 Onion, chopped
2 pounds Mussels, cleaned
½ cup White Wine
1 Garlic Clove, crushed
½ cup Water

Directions:

Heat the oil in your Crock Pot Express on MEAT/STEW and cook the onion and garlic for 3 minutes.

Add wine and cook for 1 more minute.

Place the mussels in the steaming basket and close the lid.

Cook for 2 minutes. Let the pressure drop naturally.

Duck Legs with Dried Apples

(Prep + Cook Time: 60 minutes / Servings: 4)

Ingredients:

4 Duck Leg Quarters
1 cup chopped dried apples
1 ¼ cup White Wine
1 Yellow Onions, chopped
2 tbsp grated Ginger
1 tbsp Olive Oil
Salt and Pepper, to taste

Directions:

Heat the oil in your Crock Pot Express.

Sprinkle the duck with salt and pepper and brown on all sides. Transfer to a plate. Add onions and cook for 2 minutes.

Add ginger and cook for another minute Pour the wine over and deglaze the bottom. Add apples and duck. Close the lid and cook for 45 minutes on MEAT/ STEW.

Release the pressure naturally.

Holiday Spareribs

(Prep + Cook Time: 35 minutes / Servings: 6)

Ingredients:

3 pounds Spareribs, cut
18 ounces canned Pineapple
1 cup sliced Onions
½ tsp Garlic Salt
1/3 cup Tamari Sauce
2 tbsp Apple Cider Vinegar
½ cup Tomato Paste
3 tsp Olive Oil
¼ tsp Ginger Powder
¼ tsp Pepper

Directions:

Heat the oil in your Crock Pot Express and cook the onions until tender. Add the remaining ingredients and close the lid. Cook for 20 minutes on MEAT/STEW.

Release the pressure naturally and serve.

Party Duck Bites

(Prep + Cook Time: 25 minutes / Servings: 6)

Ingredients:

1 ½ pounds Duck, cut up
1/3 cup Maple Syrup
1/3 cup Tomato Puree
1 ½ cups Water
2 tsp Basil
Salt and Pepper, to taste

Sauce:

1/3 cup Sour Cream
½ cup chopped Parsley
¼ cup Olive Oil
2 tbsp Lemon Juice
2 Jalapenos, chopped
1 Garlic Clove

Directions:

Pour the water in the Crock Pot Express and place the duck a baking pan. Stir in all duck ingredients.

Close the lid and cook on MEAT/STEW for 15 minutes.

Release the pressure naturally.

Pulse all the sauce ingredients in a food processor and transfer to a small serving bowl.

Serve the duck bites with the sauce.

Honey and Balsamic Holiday Brussel Sprouts

(Prep + Cook Time: 20 minutes / Servings: 4)

Ingredients:

1 pound Brussel Sprouts
4 Bacon Slices, cooked and crumbled
1 tsp Balsamic Vinegar
1 tbsp Honey
¼ cup chopped Walnuts

Directions:

Pour 1 ½ cups water in the Crock Pot Express and place the Brussel sprouts in the steaming basket.

Close the lid and cook on MEAT/STEW for 3 minutes.

Release the pressure naturally and transfer the sprouts to a bowl.

Drizzle with honey and balsamic vinegar and top with bacon and walnuts.

Rice Custard with Hazelnuts

(Prep + Cook Time: 30 minutes / Servings: 3)

Ingredients:

1 cup Rice
4 tbsp chopped Hazelnuts
1 tsp Vanilla Paste
1 Egg plus 1 Yolk
½ cup Sultanas
1/2 tsp Anise Seed
1 cup Milk
¼ cup Sugar
1/3 tsp Hazelnut Extract

Directions:

Pour 1 ½ cups water in the Cooking Pot.

Mix together all the ingredients in a baking dish.

Place the baking dish inside the Crock Pot Express and cover with foil.

Close the lid and cook on RICE/RISOTTO for 25 minutes.

Release the pressure naturally and serve.

Blue Cheese and Bacon Polenta Squares

(Prep + Cook Time: 80 minutes / Servings: 6)

Ingredients:

2 cups Polenta
6 Bacon Slices, cooked and crumbles
1 Onion, chopped
2 ounces Blue Cheese, crumbled
2 tsp Rosemary
1 tsp Thyme
4 cups Stock
1 tbsp Oil
½ tsp minced Garlic
Salt and Pepper, to taste

Directions:

Heat the oil in your Crock Pot Express and cook the onions until soft, on BROWN/ SAUTÉ.

Add garlic and cook for another minute.

Stir in the thyme, rosemary, stock, polenta, and season with salt and pepper.

Close the lid and cook for 10 minutes.

Release the pressure naturally.

Stir in the cheese and bacon.

Place in a lined baking pan and refrigerate for 1 hour.

Cut into squares and serve.

Carrot and Coconut Cake

(Prep + Cook Time: 65 minutes / Servings: 8)

Ingredients:

½ cup Coconut Flakes
¾ cup shredded Carrots
4 tbsp chopped Almonds
1 cup Sugar
½ tsp Nutmeg
1/3 tsp cardamom
1 cup Flour
1 Egg plus 1 Egg Yolk
1 tsp Baking Powder
1 Butter Stick
¼ tsp Baking Soda
¼ tsp Cinnamon

Directions:

Combine the dry ingredients in one bowl and whisk the wet ones in another.

Gently combine the two mixtures. Stir in the carrots and coconut. Pour this mixture in a greased baking pan.

Pour 1 ½ cups water in your Crock Pot Express and lower the trivet.

Place the baking dish inside and close the lid. Cook on MEAT/STEW for 1 hour.

Release the pressure naturally and serve.

Christmas Egg Custard

(Prep + Cook Time: 20 minutes / Servings: 4)

Ingredients:

1 Egg plus 2 Yolks
1 ½ cups Milk
2 cups Heavy Cream
½ tsp Rum Extract
¾ cup Sugar
1 tsp Anise Seeds

Directions:

Beat the eggs and yolks in a bowl,

Beat in the milk, rum, and heavy cream,

Whisk in the star anise and sugar.

Divide the mixture among 4 ramekins.

Pour 1 ½ cups water in the Crock Pot Express.

Place the ramekins inside.

Close the lid and cook for 10 minutes on MEAT/STEW.

Release the pressure naturally.

Candied Holiday Yams

(Prep + Cook Time: 10 minutes / Servings: 4)

Ingredients:

3 Yams, peeled and cubed
4 tbsp Butter
¼ cup Maple Syrup
1 cup Water
½ cup Brown Sugar
1 tsp Cinnamon
2 ½ tbsp Cornstarch
½ cup chopped Pecans
Pinch of Salt

Directions:

Combine all of the ingredients in the Crock Pot Express.

Close the lid and cook on MEAT/STEW for 5 minutes.

Release the pressure naturally and serve.

Enjoy!

Festive Rosemary Chicken

(Prep + Cook Time: 55 minutes / Servings: 4)

Ingredients:

1 Whole Chicken
1 tbsp Cayenne Pepper
2 Rosemary Sprigs
2 Garlic Cloves, crushed
¼ Onion
1 tsp dried Rosemary
Salt and Pepper, to taste
1 ½ cups Chicken Broth

Directions:

Wash and pat dry the chicken.

Season with salt, pepper, rosemary, and cayenne pepper. Rub the spices well into the meat.

Place the onion, garlic, and rosemary sprig inside the chicken's cavity.

Place the chicken in the Crock Pot Express.

Pour the broth around the chicken (not over).

Cook for 30 minutes on MEAT/STEW.

Let the pressure drop naturally.

Party Crab Legs

(Prep + Cook Time: 20 minutes / Servings: 4)

Ingredients:

1 ½ pounds frozen Crab Legs
2 tbsp melted Butter
1 cup Veggie Broth
½ cup White Wine

Directions:

Pour the broth and wine into the Crock Pot Express.

Place the crab legs in the steaming basket.

Close the lid and cook for 4 minutes on MEAT/STEW.

Release the pressure naturally.

Serve drizzled with butter.

Fancy Shrimp Scampi

(Prep + Cook Time: 45 minutes / Servings: 4)

Ingredients:

2 tbsp Butter
1 tbsp grated Parmesan Cheese
2 Shallots, chopped
¼ cup White Wine
1 tsp minced Garlic
2 tbsp Lemon Juice
1 pound Shrimp, peeled and deveined

Directions:

Melt the butter in the Crock Pot Express on BROWN/SAUTÉ and cook the shallots until soft.

Add garlic and cook for 1 more minute.

Stir in the wine and cook for another minute.

Add the remaining ingredients and stir to combine.

Close the lid and cook for 2 minutes.

Release the pressure naturally.

Serve on a platter with your favorite dipping sauce.

Author's Note

Thank you very much for purchasing this book. I am sure you have enjoyed reading it and you have made some delicous meals in your Crock Pot Express Mult-cooker.

I hope you are 100% satisfied with your premium cookbook!

And if you are, I would kindly ask you to take just 30 seconds of your time to switch this to a "Customer Review" that will help other people make the right decision and get this amazing cookbook that will help them to make the recipes they always wamted to make - just like you did! If you have already left a review, then color me impressed.....you are faster than me!

Otherwise, all you have to do is to log into your Amazon account, click "My Orders", then click "Leave a Product Review" and share your experience!

Your reviews are crucial to us and will help us improve a lot!

Thank you so much to share this journey with me!

77584669R00112

Made in the USA
Lexington, KY
29 December 2017